# My Own Miracle

ROBERT W. LITTKE, PH.D.

WestBow
PRESS®
A DIVISION OF THOMAS NELSON
& ZONDERVAN

WestBow Press books may be ordered through booksellers or by contacting:

WestBow Press
A Division of Thomas Nelson & Zondervan
1663 Liberty Drive
Bloomington, IN 47403
www.westbowpress.com
1 (866) 928-1240

ISBN: 978-1-5127-5013-3 (sc)
ISBN: 978-1-5127-5014-0 (hc)
ISBN: 978-1-5127-5012-6 (e)

Library of Congress Control Number: 2016911593

Print information available on the last page.

WestBow Press rev. date: 08/23/2016

Dr. Robert W. Littke accepted Christ at the age of twenty-two. He holds a PhD in counseling psychology. He is a commissioned minister in the Wesleyan Church and is presently on staff at Light and Life Wesleyan Church in Three Rivers, Michigan. He lives in southern Michigan with his wife, Jennifer, and has one daughter and a grandson. For twenty-five years he has been the president and CEO of one of the largest companies in America that provides services to help older adults remain independently in their own homes.

In addition, Dr. Littke worked for over twelve years in radio and television broadcasting, is a highly trained scuba diver who holds the ratings of rescue diver and Divemaster, has worked for over forty years as a deputy sheriff for the county sheriff's department, is an FAA-licensed pilot with almost thirty-five years of flying experience, was appointed by Governor John Engler to the Michigan Commission on Services to the Aging, and has served as president of both his local United Way Directors Council as well as the Michigan Directors of Services to the Aging.

All scripture quotations are taken from the King James Version (KJV) of the Bible as well as the New International Version (NIV) New King James Version (NKJV) and the New Living Translation (NLT).

To my wife, Jenny, without whose love and support this book would never have been written. You are the answer to my prayers, the one who God created just for me. You are the desires of my heart.

*Delight yourself in the Lord, and he will give you the desires of your heart.*

—Psalm 37:4 New King James Version

*That it might be fulfilled which was spoken by Esaias [Isaiah] the prophet, saying, Himself took our infirmities and bare our sicknesses.*

—Matthew 8:17 King James Version

# CONTENTS

# PREFACE

## First Things First

HEALING IS ONE OF THE most controversial subjects we can raise in the church today. The Bible is filled with accounts of Jesus's healings and other types of miracles. In this book, I pray that God will guide me in documenting His miracles today while also removing some of the stigmas attached to the topic. I pray that God will let me take you on a faith journey that will lead to your own miracles and to a very personal experience with God.

I'll assume that you are reading this book because you are now searching, as I once was, for your own miracle. God understands exactly what you are going through *at this very moment*, and while your situation may seem hopeless, *nothing* is impossible for God: *Jesus looked at them intently and said, 'Humanly speaking, it is impossible. But with God everything is possible.*[1]

If you are like me, you'll be tempted to just skip to the last chapter and find the answer to obtaining your miracle, but I warn you not to do that. This book is not about uncovering a lost set of instructions that lead to a miracle; it is about a journey that you can take to *your* own miracle, just as I did.

Perhaps as you read this you feel alone, hurt, hopeless, and abandoned, but God is right there with you, and He understands.

---

[1] Matt. 19:26 (New Living Testament), emphasis added.

God promises that *He will not leave you or forsake you.*[2] God sees your tears, He feels your heartache, and He longs to comfort you. Imagine that: the same God who spoke the world into existence loves you so much that at this moment He is focused on you. Trust me when I say that each of us faces our battles differently, and each of His beloved is hounded by a crafty adversary who would rather see us wander through life afraid of what's around the next corner than trust in God to eliminate the very thing that we are afraid of.

While I believe that God can and will heal anyone, I would be remiss if I began this book any other way than to begin by telling you of a miracle that is available to you right now that is far greater than your physical healing, the miracle of salvation.

Jesus's sacrifice for our sins (yours and mine) is so great that it cost God the highest price ever paid for anything or anyone. That sacrifice made possible the assurance that when your life here on earth is over, you can count on an eternity with Him in heaven.

While you don't have to accept Jesus to receive His miracle in your body, why would you ask for one miracle that is temporal without also accepting a far greater *eternal* miracle that is available to you right now?

I believe that it is no accident that this book is in your hands at this moment in time. The same God who created you loves you more than you will ever know or be able to comprehend. And it is He who is calling out to you at this very moment, though you may think it is you who is reaching out for Him!

God loves you so much that He sent His only Son, Jesus Christ, to die in your place so that you could have the miracle of forgiveness of all of your sins. If you are willing to repent, which means to "turn from," your sins and accept the sacrifice that He has already promised you in His Son, Jesus, you will be forgiven.

If you are feeling that God can't forgive you of the sins you are guilty of, *He can*, and He will! No sin is so severe or so great that He

---

[2] Deut. 31:6 (King James Version).

cannot erase it with the blood that Jesus shed on the cross for you. I too felt unworthy and undeserving of His love and forgiveness, but be assured that the same God who can give you the miracle you seek today can forgive and cleanse you from all the sin in your life if you'll just pray with sincerity to Him for His forgiveness.

The scriptures tell us a wonderful story about the pureness of Jesus's intent to save us. In Mark, Jesus says, "I came not to call the righteous, but sinners to repentance," and that includes you and me![3]

God's grace is greater than anything we have done, and it is by His grace that we are set free from the weight of our sin.

Right now, before you begin to read this book in search of a miracle for your body, why not accept an even greater miracle for your eternal soul by accepting Jesus Christ as your Lord and Savior? Nowhere in scripture is there a specific prayer that details what we need to say to accept Jesus as our Savior, because what is needed is not a series of words or a prayer but rather an acceptance of Christ as your personal Savior and a commitment to turning in a new direction. I have had the great honor and blessing of leading many in accepting Christ, and I would consider it an honor to lead you *right now!* Don't delay; Jesus is calling you at this very moment. The scriptures admonish us not to wait, because none of us is promised tomorrow. In 2 Corinthians 6:2 we read, "behold, *now* is the day of salvation."[4] God's grace is greater than anything we have done, and it's by His grace that we are set free from the weight of our sin.

While there are no particular words you need to say, here is one way that you can pray to accept Christ and be forgiven of all your sin. Simply pray, with a sincere heart, "Lord, I know that I have sinned and that You cannot allow my sin into Your presence. So, Lord, I repent and turn from my sin and ask You to forgive me. Your word tells me that *all have sinned* and come short of your glory, and I believe in your promise that if I "confess with my mouth the Lord

---

[3] Mark 2:17 (KJV).
[4] (KJV), emphasis added.

Jesus, and believe in my heart that you [God] raised Him from the dead," that I will be saved.[5] Lord, I do believe in and confess Jesus, and I invite Him into my heart as I accept Him right now as my Lord and my Savior. Help me now, Lord, as I accept the miracle of salvation. Walk with me as I begin my new journey with You, and teach me Your way. I love You, Lord, and I thank You for loving me and forgiving me. In Jesus's name, I pray. Amen!"

If you prayed this prayer from your heart, congratulations! You have just received the greatest miracle of all from God! Your name is now written down in the Lamb's book of life, and the angels in heaven are rejoicing.[6]

Now on to *your own* miracle!

---

[5] Rom. 3:23, 10:9 (KJV), emphasis added.
[6] Rev. 21:27.

# MEDICAL DISCLAIMER

T HROUGHOUT THE AGES, GOD HAS used healthcare professionals, modern medicine, and His authority to heal the human body. This wonderful partnership shows His divine nature and ability to use His wisdom and the hands of doctors and other healthcare professionals to accomplish healing. The information included in this publication is not intended nor implied to be a substitute for professional medical advice. The reader should always consult with his or her healthcare provider to determine the personal appropriateness of this information as well as to ask questions regarding the reader's medical conditions or treatment plans.

If you are willing, God will make you able. As the Bible says, "Now unto him that is able to do exceeding abundantly above all that we ask or think, according to the power that worketh in us, Unto him be glory in the church by Christ Jesus throughout all ages, world without end. Amen."[7]

---

[7] Eph. 3:30–21 (KJV).

# ACKNOWLEDGMENTS

I WANT TO ACKNOWLEDGE THREE PEOPLE, Sam and Becky Maddox, who helped me in the research and development of this book. They are my pastors as well as my friends, and they both set aside countless hours of their time to help me research scripture, to read and reread the drafts of this book, and to provide me with the counsel that only good friends and devoted pastors can. And, I want to thank my cousin Robert Jungiewicz as he trusted me and taught me through his challenge and on his journey. Thank you, Sam, Becky and Robert. As the Bible says, "I thank my God every time I remember you. In all my prayers for all of you, I always pray with joy because of your partnership in the gospel from the first day until now, being confident of this, that he who began a good work in you will carry it on to completion until the day of Christ Jesus."[8]

---

[8] Phil. 1:3–6 (New International Version).

# INTRODUCTION

*My Own Miracle* is the story of my journey of faith after I was faced with the devastating news of an incurable disease, and it is proof that the God of the Bible is still in the miracle-working business today.

Having read hundreds of testimonies of other people being healed, I wondered if it was actually possible for me to receive healing as well. The name of this book, then, comes from my journey to find *my own miracle*.

After having accepted Christ as a young adult, I spent decades reading the word of God (the Holy Bible). I often wondered if the stories I had read of famous men and women of God who professed to have the gifts of healing (as described in 1 Corinthians 12:4–11) really were true. I also sought evidence that God still works those same kinds of miracles today. In fact, I began a faith journey to learn the answer to one question: Would God show Himself to me with an unmistakable, undeniable, and miraculous personal physical healing?

It is only natural to wonder at some time in our Christian walks whether the promises of God apply to us in modern times, especially as they relate to miracles, healings, and spiritual gifts. *My Own Miracle* documents my journey from the doctor's phone call that dark day in October 2011 to the date when the answer to my question came. In obedience to the leading of the Holy Spirit, I began writing this book *before* I experienced healing or any indication that healing had begun. In fact, over 90 percent of this book was written before God showed me a miracle!

But Why Me, God?

It is important to preface this book with perhaps the most commonly asked question that Christians struggle with: "Why does God allow suffering in His children?" Probably every pastor out there has been asked this question many times.

It is critical to remember that God's original creation, as detailed in the creation story of Genesis, had no sickness in it. It was only when sin entered that sickness began, and it was not God who introduced sin and sickness into His creation. He has dealt with sin's effects since that time and will continue to do so until that time when we are totally separated from the sin that remains on earth and are safely home with Him.

Because of sin's effects on God's creation, He cannot promise His children a walk through this life without trials. What God can do is take us through the trials and assure us that He will be there with us. God promises His presence: "He will never leave us or forsake us."[9] He also pledges to set limits to the trials.[10] Because of this assurance of His mercy, we are sustained by His sustaining grace as we walk through this life, and we are confident of our victory through Jesus Christ.

God promises that if we place our faith and trust in Him, one day we will pass beyond the trials of this life and arrive safely home on the other side, where He is waiting for us. In the time between now and then, God is still showing Himself to be faithful.

This book is evidence that the God of the Universe cares about every believer *just as much* as He cared for those Jesus healed in the Bible and that He loves each of us equally.[11] The ministry of Jesus, as He walked on the face of the earth in the gospels, is still alive, active,

---

[9] Deut. 31:6 (KJV).
[10] 1 Cor. 10:13.
[11] Acts 10:34.

and available to His children today! Our God is a personal God who desires a personal relationship with each one of His children.

One thing that I clearly learned on my journey is that God does not heal in a prescribed way. Just as each one of us is His unique creation, so too are His wondrous ways of granting miracles and healings.

CHAPTER 1

# WHAT IS HAPPENING TO ME?

## Something Is Just Not Right

WE ALL KNOW WHAT'S NORMAL in our own bodies, and no one knows our bodies better than we do. My story begins in 2008, when I first noticed a faint but persistent tremor in my right hand. Actually, I have had tremors since I was young, but this was in addition to that. I first noticed the change as I walked from my car into my office.

I prided myself on staying in shape and would purposely park my car in the employee parking lot that is farthest from the building where my office is located. I had a personal conviction that it was better to leave the parking spaces closer to the front door for our older clients and those with disabilities. This was especially important since the organization I worked for provided services to the frailest elderly clients in our community.

As I made the walk from my car to the office building that day, I began noticing a strange pulsating sensation in my right hand. At first I dismissed it as just a part of aging, but as the months went by, it did not subside. In fact, it became more noticeable.

I also worked on a part-time basis for my local sheriff's department as a deputy, especially if there were large events that required more help than usual. I noticed the tremor while working there as well.

1

It started as nothing more than a simple twitching in one finger, but it gradually progressed over the years to a noticeable tremor that became so severe that I could no longer bluff my way through another round of firearms qualification, which I was required to do twice per year.

I will never forget the day the sheriff walked in shortly after being sworn into office. He came into the room where some other deputies and I were having a meeting to swear us in as well. As he said, "Raise your right hands," I sheepishly attempted to raise mine, only to have it instantly begin to shake. Being that the sheriff was a personal friend of mine, he proceeded to read the lengthy oath, asking each of us to repeat it back to him. I tried everything I could to dampen the tremor. As I stood there embarrassed, I knew that my career in law enforcement was soon to be over.

I left that meeting and quickly went to the locker room, where I emptied out my locker. It broke my heart to pull the faded name tag off my locker. "Sgt. Bob Littke," it read. Within a week I wrote a resignation letter and submitted it to the sheriff without mention of the incident—or the tremor—because I was too embarrassed and ashamed to explain it to him. Then, with a huge lump in my throat, I dropped the letter into the mailbox. I knew I was ending a chapter in my life.

In my leadership role in the organization where I worked full-time as president and CEO, I was routinely asked to speak to large groups to explain what our organization did, how it helped those in need, and the role it played in supporting older adults to maintain themselves safely in their own homes for as long as possible. Now in my mid-fifties, I began noticing that the shaking I saw in those we cared for was becoming a part of me—and not a welcome part at that.

As I would take the podium before staff meetings, luncheon crowds, or church audiences, I would become self-conscious that they could see that the notes in my hand were shaking. And I knew from working in the broadcast industry earlier in my life that the shaking had nothing to do with fear; public speaking had always come naturally to me. I can honestly say that I can talk just as comfortably to two hundred people as I can to two.

All the rationalizations and excuses were beginning to come into play: perhaps I was drinking too much caffeine, not getting enough sleep, under too much stress, working too hard, and so on.

## The Process of Discovery

Having overcome thyroid cancer some years earlier, I knew that denial was no way to address symptoms that persisted and—in my case—were growing worse. I turned to a trusted friend, who is also my personal physician, for both treatment and counsel. As in the past, he proved to be wise in both regards. He began the long and arduous process of finding a cause. He had found my thyroid cancer very early on in its development almost ten years earlier (which I am now totally cured of, thanks to medical science, a team of good doctors, and the healing power of God), but now I was faced with a far less identifiable foe. Unlike cancer or other diseases, neurological issues, such as tremors, are far more difficult to diagnose and often can go on for years without a diagnostic label.

After several attempts to utilize local specialists to determine the cause of my tremors, I asked if there would be a benefit to seeing a specialist somewhere else. My doctor readily agreed to send me to a movement-disorders clinic at the university hospital in a nearby city.

In September 2011 I met with a personable young physician who was serving his residency at the university clinic. In partnership with older and more experienced neurologists, he conducted a complete neurological evaluation. After completing his initial workup, he and his team were able to narrow down the possibilities to two possible causes: a benign essential tremor or Parkinson's disease.

Having had slight tremors as far back as I could recall, I was aware of benign essential tremor and had some limited knowledge of it. In fact, my earliest recollection of visiting our family doctor as a child included my mother asking if my shaking was normal or not. He was an old-school country doctor, and I distinctly recall his response that some people just shake.

Only those who have gone through a modern-day medical workup, such as the one that I was going through with this young doctor, can describe the fear and anxiety of an entire future being placed in peril. If the diagnosis would be a benign essential tremor, meaning a hand or body tremor that has no known cause or disease associated with it, then the long-term prognosis would be to live with an annoying tremor that does not limit life expectancy or necessarily result in a disabling condition. Katharine Hepburn, for example, who starred in countless movies, including *On Golden Pond* in 1981, is one of the most notable celebrities who had an essential tremor.[12]

If the diagnosis would be Parkinson's disease, the story would be quite different, and the prognosis would be far more devastating. According to the Cleveland Clinic, Parkinson's disease is defined as "a chronic progressive neurological disease that affects nerve cells (neurons) in an area of the brain near the neck, known as the substantia nigra."[13] This area of the brain normally produces dopamine, a chemical called a neurotransmitter that transmits signals between areas in the brain. These signals, when working normally, coordinate smooth and balanced muscle movement. Parkinson's disease causes these neurons to die, leading to a lack of dopamine in the brain, especially in the part of the brain known as the basal ganglia. The basal ganglia are responsible for organizing movement and commands from other parts of the brain, so the loss of dopamine causes patients to gradually lose the ability to control their body movements.

[12] Barclay, Laurie, "Don't Be Embarrassed by Essential Tremors," WebMD, 2001, http://www.webmd.com/brain/news/20010606/dont-be-embarrassed-by-essential-tremors.
[13] "Parkinson's Disease: An Overview," last modified 2015, https://my.clevelandclinic.org/health/diseases_conditions/hic_Parkinsons_Disease_An_Overview.

Approximately one million Americans have Parkinson's disease, and more than fifty thousand Americans are diagnosed with Parkinson's disease each year. At the time of writing, Parkinson's has *no* cure. It is degenerative, meaning that it only gets worse. If the person with it lives long enough, Parkinson's will lead to total or near total disability.

# CHAPTER 2

# THE STORY BEGINS

O<small>N</small> O<small>CTOBER</small> 7, 2011, <small>ONLY</small> days shy of my fifty-eighth birthday, my cell phone rang while I was at work. The doctor who had conducted my evaluation was calling to give me the results of the tests he had run on me.

At first the conversation took a lighter tone, but it quickly took a serious turn when he dropped the bomb. He informed me that the results, which he stressed were not absolute, did seem to indicate that I might have Parkinson's disease. From that point on, all I really heard was "Parkinson's disease."

In his attempt to soften the blow, the doctor immediately spoke about research that might someday lead to a cure. As he struggled to find some words of encouragement, he added, "Remember, you don't die *from* Parkinson's; you die *with* Parkinson's." While I know he was trying his best to put a positive spin on the devastating news, this bombshell could not have been softened by anything he could have said. Having worked with Parkinson's patients for decades, I had seen firsthand the devastation this horrible disease can cause.

Being the analytical type, I immediately embarked upon researching the latest information, periodicals, study trials, and discoveries, only to get more depressed with each item I called up on the Internet. Article after article spoke of the extreme complexity of this disease and the unlikelihood that a cure would be found in the next decade. Even if a cure were to be found soon, it would take years for it to go through the complex testing processes and trials required before it could be brought to the public. My fear, anxiety, and feelings of hopelessness were growing. What would I do next? How could I tell my wife and family? And for that matter, *what* could I tell them with this vague diagnosis? And was the doctor even right? Did I even have Parkinson's? After all, he could not confirm it!

## My Process of Acceptance

In her famous book *On Death and Dying*, Elisabeth Kübler-Ross defines the five stages of grief.[14] These stages mirror those that a person goes through when given a catastrophic diagnosis. As a psychologist, I closely observed myself as the steps unfolded.

### Step 1: Denial

In this first step our minds help us attempt (in an illogical way) to survive. Everything else seems meaningless, and life becomes overwhelming. For someone without Christ, this stage can be catastrophic. For me it was a time to say, "This is *not* happening to me" or "That new test they used on me must be faulty" or "My symptoms don't *exactly* match with a diagnosis of Parkinson's," and so on.

During this denial period I began to reread every book in my library on scriptural healing, and I searched the Internet with every search term imaginable as I began the journey toward *My Own Miracle*. The most discouraging thing was that there was no immediate fix and no hope of a cure in the near future.

It wasn't long before I felt hopelessness setting in, especially as I saw a pattern developing. Anytime I found some potential cure, it was always followed by a disclaimer that "clinical trials had not yet begun" and that any reasonable expectation for a cure available to

---

[14] "Elisabeth Kübler-Ross Biography," *Biography*, http://www.biography.com/people/elisabeth-kubler-ross-262762.

the general public was at least ten years off, if ever. Many reputable sources literally said that the reason there had not yet been a cure was that modern medical science couldn't even guarantee it understood the cause of this devastating disease called Parkinson's.

To be totally honest, this denial stage is one that I slipped in and out of many times for years. This stage was and still is, as of the time of writing, an easy one to drift into because of the vagueness of my diagnosis. When I first entered this stage I wondered if I really had Parkinson's or if this was actually an essential tremor. Even when my wife went with me to follow-up appointments, we would leave feeling as though something was missing, which did not help. As time went on I began to suspect that others did not believe me when they would ask questions, such as "What did the doctor say?" or "What do you mean you are not sure?" While each of these questions is valid, they only forced me deeper into the denial stage rather than help me avoid it or move on.

*Thank goodness for strong godly people!* I was brought back to my senses by a family member who pointed out to me the error of succumbing to any diagnosis that was as vague as mine. I will never forget her admonition to not "speak into existence that which has not yet been confirmed." If you have anyone in your life (believer or not) who is trying to tell you that you have a condition that your doctor has not yet confirmed, remind the person that this is not helping you as you face your challenge.

### Step 2: Anger

Satan loves to use anger at every opportunity he can, and in this second step he tries to use it against us. We actually must go through this step, since anger is a necessary stage in the process toward ultimate acceptance. Like everything else the enemy does, he uses our natural emotions to cause even more harm.

It is thought that the more you allow yourself to feel, the more you can move toward healing and acceptance. Anger, however, is an emotion, and like other emotions, it must be managed. If we are totally honest, anger has *no* limits, and it can be damaging when it is focused on those we love most, including family, friends, and even God.

Many books have been penned that ask the same basic questions: "Why?," "Why *me*?," "Why did this happen when I don't deserve this?," "Where is God in all of this?," and "Why is God allowing this in my life?" Perhaps the most damaging questions that we ask in anger are "What did I do to cause this?" and "What do I have to do to get God to take this away from me?"

The devil is a master at mixing up ghastly concoctions that serve only to sicken God's children when they are at their weakest. He begins by using anger, compounds it with pain, and adds in a large dose of confusion; then he tops it all off with a feeling of abandonment. Does this sound familiar? While it makes no sense to a healthy mind that we would lash out at those we love during a trial, the devil confounds the mind with impossible scenarios and misinformation that can cause us to compound the problem with our actions.

I doubt that Satan created anything new when he put thoughts in my mind, such as "My family and friends don't understand what I'm going through," "They aren't there for me in the way that I need them to be," "Instead of helping me, they are only compounding my struggle," and "What's wrong with them? They're making matters worse by adding to my problems!"

If we are honest, those around us do *not* understand what we are going through, *but that does not mean they don't care* or that they don't want to help. In fact, it's probably their greatest desire to help. Overwhelming frustration comes when their attempts to help are met with anger, withdrawal, silence, or our lashing out at them. Who could blame them for stepping back or giving up when their efforts to help are met with only resistance or a cold shoulder?

One truth God gave me in the process was to picture my wife feeling helpless and hurting just as I was. Truly, during trials like this our family members and friends are feeling many of the same emotions we are. In a very real way they are even more frustrated, because they have even less control than the person they are trying to love, help, and care for.

Men especially are at a disadvantage because of the way we are wrongly taught to think. We (men) generally know far more about suppressing our anger than we do about feeling it, managing it, or understanding it.

I recall an episode of *Star Trek* in which the supposedly totally logical Mr. Spock is being put to the test. [15] If you've never seen the show, he prides himself on being totally logical and devoid of human emotions or feelings. In this episode we see him in a room surrounded by computers that are almost simultaneously firing questions at him so quickly that most people listening can hardly even understand, let alone attempt to answer. Yet Mr. Spock does so, turning to one machine after the other, quickly answering even the most complex questions. Then Mr. Spock is asked the one question that he cannot answer: "How do you feel?" The scene becomes eerily silent, as he clearly cannot comprehend the question. The computer repeats the question: "How do you feel? How do you feel? How do you feel?" As the scene draws to a close, Mr. Spock finally makes the admission that he does not understand the question.

If you are like me, this must sound familiar. My wife would be quick to remind me that I am more like Mr. Spock than she'd like me to be. I would have to agree with her that this is an area where I struggle and which can also lead to issues like anger.

Psychologists and pastors know a simple truth that we all can learn from: if we don't allow suppressed anger, fear and anxiety to come out of our mouths, it will eventually be manifested in our minds and our bodies.

Men in our society are taught to suppress their feelings and emotions, which ultimately manifests in distressing physical

---

[15] "How Do You Feel, Spock?," YouTube video, 1:24, posted by "ralplwil," November 25, 2012, https://www.youtube.com/watch?v=e5CHjiuFehU.

symptoms, such as headaches or ulcers, or in emotional problems that result in even greater frustration for them and for others around them. With all of this in mind, it becomes obvious why the devil loves to use our God-given emotions against us.

## Step 3: Bargaining

Perhaps the most unrealistic phase any of us will go through is the bargaining phase. In this phase we start playing "let's make a deal" with God. Piling one lie upon another, we attempt to rationalize that the challenge we are facing is because of something we did. We tell ourselves, "God is allowing this tragedy to enter my life because I did something to offend Him, and through this trial He's going to somehow fix me."

I struggled with this area a lot on my journey and am still tempted to go here even when I know there is no value in it because this is not how God works or thinks. While God can use trials to help us grow and mature, trials can also lead to the next big mistake as we attempt to counter a perceived *wrong* with an even stronger *right*. We rationalize to ourselves, "If I promise to devote the remainder of my life to this positive change, how could a loving God not respond in my favor?"

It is common for people to think that once this bargaining stage is completed it will not be revisited, but the reality is that it's common to come back again and again as we attempt to renegotiate with God. Only when we learn this truth can we avoid the trap of thinking that we can somehow negotiate or bargain our way out of the situation we are in. Only then will we realize that bargaining is *not* how a loving God shows His love for us.

The Bible is loaded with verses that remind us that God loves us beyond comprehension,[16] that He loves us unconditionally,[17] that

---

[16] John 3:16.
[17] Ps. 139:1.

through Christ our wrongs are forgiven,[18] and that there is no need for negotiation or bargaining since the price for our wrongs was paid once and-for-all on the cross.[19]

## Step 4: Depression

Another powerful weapon in Satan's arsenal is depression. It leads to distrust, doubt, and a myriad of other failings. After bargaining, the mind snaps squarely into the present and perceives hopelessness for the future. Emptiness moves in, and then grief takes us to deeper levels than God would ever desire for His children.

The devil knows that the depressive stage feels as though what we are facing will last forever, but by its very nature depression will rise and fall, almost on its own. While depression is understandable and actually a normal and appropriate response to a great loss, it has to be addressed and must be controlled.

Depression, especially for a Christian, must only be a step along the way. Proverbs 13:12 addresses depression by reminding us that beyond despair is *hope*: "Hope deferred makes the heart sick, but a longing fulfilled is a tree of life."[20]

## Step 5: Acceptance

The acceptance stage is where action can begin, because it is where reality begins. For Christians this also is the point at which a sixth step, surrendering it to God, can enter. To clarify, I do *not* mean one should surrender to the disease; rather, one should surrender the problem to the God who can offer hope in the face of the impossible. After all, if that which we are facing is impossible for us to handle, then why not live up to what we preach as we *let go and let God?* Matthew 11:30 reminds us that no matter what our burden

---

[18] Matt. 26:28.

[19] 1 Pet. 3:18.

[20] (NIV).

is, God desires to share it with us and to help lighten the load: "For my yoke is easy, and my burden is light."[21]

The word *surrender* is actually a military battle term. It implies giving up all rights and control. When an opposing army surrenders, it must lay down its weapons and its control from that point forward. When we surrender to God, it works in much the same way. When we surrender our bodies and our lives to God, we acknowledge that He has a plan for our lives; surrendering to Him means we set aside our own plans and seek instead His plans for us. Unlike in human-fought wars, however, the good news is that God's plan for us is always in our best interest. That is why as we go through trials, it is always best to surrender ourselves and our struggles to Him and to *His* will for us.

---

[21] (KJV).

CHAPTER 3

# Doing All the Wrong Things for (What Seem to Be) the Right Reasons

## Am I Doing the Right Thing?

I'M REMINDED OF THE WORDS of Abba Eban who said, "I'm confident that Americans will always do the right thing, after they've exhausted every other option!"[22] I can easily apply these words to my own life and my way of dealing with struggles. Why is it that if my Father is the King of Kings, I go through trials as if I were a spiritual pauper, as if I had no spiritual resources at my disposal? The vast majority of the things I tried on the journey to *My Own Miracle* were all the *wrong* things!

You'll note that a significant portion of this book deals with all the things I learned the hard way on my journey. While you may be tempted to say, "I'll just skip all the things that did *not* work and move right to the final chapter," I'd strongly advise you not to. Why? Because that is, in part, what I did as I attempted to move right to

---

[22] "Americans Will Always Do the Right Thing—After Exhausting All the Alternatives," *Quote Investigator, November 11, 2012,* http://quoteinvestigator.com/2012/11/11/exhaust-alternatives/.

14

the solution without doing all the things along the way that God would want me to do.

The natural tendency of the problem solver is to try to make the desired end results materialize as soon as possible. In my journey, God did not only allow me to stumble and fall but also, through the process, to build a basis for knowledge that I would never have built had I taken only one giant-miracle step on this faith journey. In short, God granted me a much greater blessing by taking me *through* my trial rather than simply granting me a miracle when I first asked Him for it.

Instantaneous miracles can and do still happen, but don't feel that God has abandoned you if He allows your healing to come through a process of development and discovery (which we'll discuss in more detail later). In some ways, this process is an even more precious experience than an instantaneous miracle would be because it allows us time to learn from the Master as He takes us step-by-step through a personal journey of faith with Him. Just imagine! The same God who spoke the earth and all His creation into existence is walking with *you* as your personal guide and teacher. What a great God we serve!

God wants you to develop your own foundation, built upon personal study and the strength of His word. Join me now as I take you step-by-step on the journey toward finding my (and your) own miracle. Let's begin with the mistakes I made along the way.

## My Series of Mistakes

Let me begin by saying that the mistakes listed here are placed in the order in which they occurred to me. They are not in any order of importance … mistakes are mistakes! Each one of these mistakes was the wrong choice, but each allowed God the opportunity to build my faith and my understanding of His unspeakable wisdom and love.

## Mistake 1: Expecting a Miracle the Way *I* Expect a Miracle

Miracles happen instantly, right? The true answer is that they absolutely do ... sometimes. But how can that be? After all, if you've spent any time watching Christian television, you've seen people healed instantly, right? Yes, and that is the way God works ... sometimes.

We've all seen people in prayer lines receive their miracles the very second someone prays over them, lays hands on them, or casts out demons as Jesus did, right? Yes, absolutely ... sometimes.

My first mistake was to put God into a box labeled "This is how I expect God to work." God is beyond limits, and He can choose to heal His children instantly or over time, through people or alone, in public or in private, at a healing meeting in a great church or right there in the room where you are reading this book. As I stated earlier, there is one thing I clearly learned on my journey: God does not heal in a prescribed format. You might say that this is the reason God wanted me to write this book. Over and over He has shown me how often He works miracles that people disregard as miracles because they did not happen instantly. How wrong that is! Albert Einstein is famous for saying, "There are only two ways to live your life. One is as though nothing is a miracle. The other is as though everything is a miracle."[23] We have miracles happening all around us that most of us do not see because we have not learned to see them. Just as each one of us is His unique creation, so too are each of His wondrous ways of granting healings and *other* miracles.

Perhaps one of the greatest obstacles to receiving a miracle is looking for it to appear in the way we expect a miracle to occur. All of us have read the miraculous stories in the Bible in which the lame instantly were able to walk, blinded eyes were restored to sight, or, one of the first miracles Jesus preformed, plain water was instantly turned into wine. These *are* miracles. Perhaps they are the most

---

[23] "Albert Einstein: Quotable Quotes," *Goodreads*, http://www.goodreads.com/quotes/987-there-are-only-two-ways-to-live-your-life-one.

rewarding type of miracle from the perspective of the natural mind since as soon as someone presents a need, there is an instantaneous response … a visible and instantaneous miracle!

On my journey I attended numerous healing meetings with well-known people only to go home disappointed. I don't think I will ever forget one instance in particular. After having driven across three states to get to the healing meeting, I stood before a man who had seen countless people receive undeniable healings over the life of his ministry. As I stood before him, he laid hands on me, praying for me with get fervor and … nothing! He prayed again, and the results were the same. I left the church feeling dejected after seeing so many others healed that Saturday night.

I stayed that night at a nearby hotel. Since the next morning was Sunday, I returned to his church. He ended the service by asking those who wanted to be healed to come forward, which I did. You may have already guessed what happened: the results were the same. No healing! Did that mean God was no longer in the healing business? Did it mean I would never receive healing? Did it mean there was no God and I was being foolish in believing He was there? No! That is what the devil is waiting for: a chance to put his slimy foot in the door.

God also works miracles in other ways. We must not only look for the instant and visible miracles, or we risk missing His miracle-working power in our lives. God also works miracles through time and through process. Recall for a moment the story of the fig tree to which Jesus commanded, "No man eat fruit of thee hereafter for ever."[24] Verse 14 reminds us that Jesus's disciples heard what He said but saw no immediate or instantaneous miracle. Take note also that Jesus never actually reached out and touched the tree but simply spoke a command to it: "No man [shall] eat fruit of thee hereafter forever." It was not until sometime later (most believe at least the next day) that we read what happened: "In the morning, as

---

[24] Mark 11:12–14 (KJV).

they went along, they saw the fig tree withered from the roots. Peter remembered and said to Jesus, 'Rabbi, look! The fig tree you cursed has withered!'"[25] A miracle had occurred, but it occurred through a process, through His spoken word and through His authority, over time.

The entire book of Job demonstrates a journey or process that God allowed in one of His most faithful believers. The process culminated in numerous miracles in the life of this man who so deeply loved his God and who God cherished and held up as an example of one of His best.

It is also interesting to note in the story of the fig tree that through this process and over time, Jesus was able to teach a lesson for many generations to learn from and remember. Had the tree miraculously vanished, what would the lesson be? Would it even have been mentioned in the Bible? Clearly God sometimes takes His time to work miracles so that we can learn from the experience and truly grow in our faith.

Through this process over time, Jesus used this miracle to teach His disciples about faith. Jesus teaches, "Have faith in God," and says, "Truly I tell you, if anyone says to this mountain, 'Go, throw yourself into the sea,' and does not doubt in their heart but *believes* that what they say <u>will happen</u>, it will be done for them. Therefore I tell you, whatever you ask for in prayer, believe that you have received it, *and it will be yours.*"[26]

When we limit God to only working instantaneous and visible miracles, we quite simply *limit God*!

## Mistake 2: Believing What Has Happened to Me Is Somehow My Fault

A common and easily made mistake is to believe that your situation is somehow your fault and therefore to say to yourself,

---

[25] Mark 11:20–21 (NIV).
[26] Mark 11:22–24 (NIV), emphasis added.

"God won't grant my request for a miracle until I somehow make things right."

The truth is that God hears and answers all our prayers, but He does so by His will and in His way. Therefore, the answer you receive may not be the answer you want. It's critical to remember that God loves you with all His heart. You are His creation and His child, and His decision to grant or not grant you a miracle at a given point in time is based on His perfect wisdom and love for you.

I am reminded of a prayer that I once read on the Internet. I'm not sure who wrote it, but it went like this:

> It seems that one Sunday morning at a small southern church, a new pastor called on one of his older deacons to lead in the opening prayer. The deacon stood up, bowed his head and said: "Lord, I *hate* buttermilk." The pastor opened one eye and wondered where this was going. The deacon continued, "And Lord, I hate lard." Now the pastor was totally perplexed. The deacon continued again, "And Lord, I ain't too crazy about plain flour. But after you mix 'em all together and bake 'em in a hot oven, I just *love* homemade biscuits. Lord, help us to realize when life gets hard, when things come up that we don't like, whenever we don't understand what You are doing, that we need to wait and see what You are making. After You get through mixin' and bakin', it'll probably be something even better than biscuits. Amen."

I love that story and have used it many times to illustrate the point that God looks far into the future and well past the individual issues that we face as He focuses on something much greater that He desires for us.

Since we are humans and do not have the true mind of God,

it is understandable that doubt enters when our prayers seem to go unanswered. Likewise, you may not understand why a particular situation remains and your burden is not lifted. You may not understand why, but remember that *no* does not necessarily mean *never*. Sometimes it can also mean *not now*.

Those of us who are parents have been asked for things by our children. Sometimes we will grant the request, but often we don't because we know that it's not in our child's best interest at the time. As parents we have the best intentions and love for our children, yet our children often get angry because what they're asking for makes sense from *their* perspective.

When faced with the nagging "it's my fault" stumbling block, we must pause for a moment and be thankful that God is responding in our best interest overall. He's not just saying a quick yes to make us feel better for the moment. And just because we may not understand His apparent lack of action now does not mean that we never will.

Just as in that old gospel song "Farther Along," we are reminded that "Farther along we'll know all about it, farther along we'll understand why, and we'll understand it all by and by."

## Mistake 3: Believing the Words of the Enemy

Since that first visit with Adam and Eve in the Garden of Eden, the devil has fed the church (and most believers) lies intended to defeat them. The devil will tell you that the miracles in the Bible are just stories created to entice would-be believers into the false hope that they too can receive miracles. Since the fall, he's been whispering in believers' ears, "You cannot do the same works as Jesus"; "You'll never get a miracle"; "God rewards His faithful followers, and you don't meet His standards of faithfulness"; "You haven't been a Christian long enough," "You don't know the scriptures well enough," or "You do not pray enough, love God enough, and/or aren't mature enough." On and on goes his stream of deception. In short, these are lies and not worthy of our time. In truth, all we really need to do is to yield to God's promises and believe His promises; then we leave the hard part up to Him.

## Mistake 4: Having the "Prenuptial Agreement" Mentality

Today it is common for couples considering marriage to also consider a prenuptial agreement. According to Merriam-Webster, a prenuptial agreement is "an agreement made between a man and a woman before marrying in which they give up future rights to each other's property in the event of divorce."[27] In short, it's a supposedly fail-safe effort to protect individuals from losing their possessions in the event that the marriage does not work.

As both a psychologist and a Christian, I have to ask myself if a prenuptial agreement is in fact a plan *for* failure. We as Christians need to consider our level of trust in God. After all, scripture says that faith is the substance of things *hoped* for, not things *guaranteed*.[28]

Let's consider what true faith is. Merriam-Webster defines *faith* as "a firm belief in something for which there is *no proof*."[29] Just as we must have faith in our spouses in marriage, we must have an even greater faith in the God in whom we place our eternal hope. The prenuptial fallacy says, "I'll leave myself an option if this does not work." Or, in other words, it says, "I don't have confidence or a *firm belief* that this will really work." We read the consequences of this type of thinking in James 1:8: "A double minded man is unstable in all his ways."[30]

In truth, God does not make provision for "partial faith" or for His partial gifts. Partial faith is an oxymoron. I recall someone once saying that partial faith is a total victory for Satan. The very nature

[27] *The Merriam-Webster Online Dictionary*, s.v. "prenuptial agreement," http://www.merriam-webster.com/dictionary/prenuptial%20agreement.
[28] Heb. 11:1 (KJV).
[29] *Merriam-Webster*, s.v. "faith," *http://*www.merriam-webster.com/dictionary/faith, emphasis added.
[30] (KJV).

of the concept of faith demands that we must put our total selves into God's trust.

There is no such thing as a spiritual life jacket. If there were such a thing, perhaps Peter would have put one on before stepping out of the boat when Jesus appeared to him on the water and called out to him, "Come."[31] Imagine if Peter had responded to Jesus's command by saying, "Yes, Lord, I'll come, just as soon as I put on my life jacket!" His total faith in Jesus was all that he required when faced with the impossible, and he literally stepped out in pure faith and headed for the one who could save him!

Just like Peter, we need to say to ourselves, "This makes no earthly sense and is impossible for *me* ... but God says it, so I'm stepping out in total faith to His calling."

Imagine for a moment all the parallels between the Bible and our walks in faith when we need Jesus in times of trial. In this verse of scripture, Peter is thinking that he is about to die. He sees what he thinks is "a spirit," and he cries out for fear.[32] Then Jesus says to him, "It is I; be not afraid."[33] Right now, at this very moment, imagine that Jesus is calling out to you saying, "Be not afraid. It is I. Come to me."

We too need to realize that He is there as we face life's apparently impossible challenges, no matter how hopeless the storm seems.

Later we see Peter's faith tested, which many think is where we get the phrase a "step of faith" or a "leap of faith." Jesus responds to what Peter's realization that the man before him must be Jesus. In short, Peter says, "Lord, if it's you ... tell me to come to you on the water."[34] And as simply and directly as it could be spoken, Jesus says, "Come."

You'll note that Peter, in his response, says *nothing*. He asks no further questions. He steps out of the boat in the middle of a

---

[31] Matt. 14:22–33 (KJV).
[32] Matt. 14:26.
[33] Matt. 14:27.
[34] Matt. 14:29 (NIV).

life-threatening storm. The verse says he "walked on the water and came toward Jesus."[35] Take note that he does not keep one hand on the boat, take a lifeline with him, ask himself if he knows how to swim, or tell others to stand by to rescue him if his plan fails. He recognizes that it is not a time to trust in his own abilities but a time to trust entirely in Jesus's pure and simple command to "Come."

It is only when he considers the natural event (the storm) that Peter falters and quickly realizes the foolishness of reverting to his plan B. He turns back to the one upon whom his faith is centered and cries out, "Lord, save me!"[36] Take note of how long Jesus waits to react to Peter's cries for help. In verse 31 it says Jesus "immediately … reached out his hand and caught him" and, instead of scolding him, simply asked, "Why did you doubt?"[37]

Finally, and pay close attention to this point, it is important to note that the storm does not stop when Jesus first appears or when Peter calls out to Him or when Peter steps out in faith! In fact, we are led to believe that the storm continues as Peter walks on the water, begins to sink, and cries out to Jesus, and that it still continues even as Jesus reaches out and saves him. In a modern world where we expect things to happen instantly (if not sooner), it is important to remind ourselves that when we reach out in faith, sometimes God allows the storm to continue, even when He has already begun to work a miracle. In fact, from the moment Peter and the others saw Jesus on the water near their boat … the miracle had *already begun*. It is only when "they climbed into the boat that the wind died down."[38] They then realize the miracle that they had just witnessed and give thanks saying, "Truly you are the Son of God."[39]

---

[35] Matt. 14:29 (NIV).

[36] Matt. 14:30.

[37] (NIV).

[38] Matt. 14:32 (NIV).

[39] Matt. 14:33 (NIV).

## Mistake 5: The "I'll Give It a Try" Trap

How often in life does someone give us a suggestion and we respond with a casual "Alright, I'll give that a try"? Nowhere in scripture will you find such a casual commitment that succeeds. While we commonly use this statement, its real meaning couldn't be more obvious.

We would probably be more honest if we said, "I have little faith, but what do I have to lose? I'll give that a try!" Faith is the "confidence in what we hope for and assurance about what we do not see."[40] Imagine if that verse said, "Faith doesn't account for much because I don't have faith in what I cannot see." Yet that is what we do when we read God's promises in the Bible and say halfheartedly, "I'll give it a try!"

One reoccurring theme I've always found in scripture is that God honors our faith. Just as a child must place faith in what the parent says in order to learn, we too must honor our heavenly Father's wisdom through our faith in Him.

In scripture, God always asks His people to do what they can do on their own as their faithful contribution toward the accomplishment of a miracle. Over and over we see Jesus ask people to do what they can do before He works a miracle. To make my point, here is a partial list:

- Jesus turns water into wine at the marriage in Cana of Galilee. Notice that before He does this He asks them to "fill the jars with water"; this is the part *they* can do in the miracle.[41]
- Peter walks on water. Jesus does not come to Peter. He asked Peter to come to Him. Jesus wants Peter to show that

---

[40] Heb. 11:1 (NIV).
[41] John 2:7 (KJV).

he trusts Him, and He asks Peter to do what Peter can do: "Come."[42]

- Jesus heals a woman with an issue of blood. She chooses to do what she can do to receive her miracle when she reaches out to touch the hem of His garment.[43]

- Jesus raises Lazarus from the dead. Before He enters the tomb, He asks others to roll the stone away. When Jesus rises from the dead, He doesn't need help rolling the stone away. Once again we see Him say (to paraphrase), "Do your part, show your faith, and then I'll do the miracle that you cannot do on your own."[44]

- Jesus creates the miracle of the loaves and fishes. Jesus asks the disciples to give Him the five loaves and two fishes that they have. He demonstrates that even when we don't think we have enough, we still need to *give Him what we have*. Then He'll bless and multiply it.[45] We see this concept demonstrated many other times in scripture, such as in the parable of the mustard seed.[46]

- And then there's the lesson Jesus teaches to Simon. Simon has been fishing all night without catching anything. Then he does what he can do, and he does it the way Jesus says. When he shows his faith this way, he gets his miracle and catches so many fish that his boat begins to sink.[47]

The point I'm making here is that we cannot simply ask for a miracle and then sit back and wait for it to be served to us. We need to ask, "God, what do you want me to do? How would you like me to demonstrate my faith, God?" And if you don't feel you have the

---

[42] Matt. 14:29 (KJV).
[43] Luke 8:43–48 (KJV).
[44] John 11:38–44 (KJV).
[45] John 6:1–14 (KJV).
[46] Matt. 13:31–35 (KJV).
[47] Luke 5:1–22 (KJV).

faith to ask for or receive a miracle, take a lesson from the father who was asking for a miracle for his child: "The father of the child cried out, and said in tears, Lord, I believe; help thou mine unbelief."[48] He got his miracle!

## Mistake 6: Having an "I Want My Miracle *Now*" Attitude

We've all heard that funny old line: "Lord, teach me to be patient, and please hurry!" Scripture tells us that "my thoughts are not your thoughts, neither are your ways my ways, saith the Lord."[49] In an age of instant gratification and microwave meals, why shouldn't we expect to see miracles happen as soon as we desire them? Most of us have seen healing lines at miracle services, and that's great, but what if God chooses to delay your miracle?

Have you ever stepped up to an elevator as I have and seen someone repeatedly pushing the button, as if doing so is somehow going to make the elevator car arrive faster? While this might seem silly, I have done it. Have you? That is the same way we often approach God when we ask for the miracles we seek: "Hurry up, God! Did you forget about me, God? How many times are you going to make me ask, God?"

While it's easy to scoff at Thomas (doubting Thomas), it's hard not to identify with his failures of faith in the Bible. Did you ever ask yourself, "Why does the author of the gospel of John tell this story?" After all, it is not exactly a story of great faith! The gospel has just related the appearance of Jesus to His disciples and confirms that indeed Jesus showed them "his hands and his side."[50] Note that He does not show Thomas only; He shows *them*. The gospel of John has already verified the miraculous resurrection of Jesus, so why tell a story about Thomas's doubt?

The verse at the end of this story provides us with an answer.

---

[48] Mark 9:24 (KJV).
[49] Isaiah 55:8 (KJV).
[50] John 20:20 (KJV).

In John 20:29, Jesus says, "Thomas, because thou hast seen me, thou hast believed: blessed are they that have not seen, and yet have believed."[51] The story of Thomas is addressed to those who *have not seen*. Here Jesus is teaching others that were not at His crucifixion and who might be questioning His resurrection. The gospel clearly tells us that seeing and believing is good, but that our faith is what can bless us far more than any proof.

As humans who base everything in linear thought, a type of thinking that follows a step-by-step process, we have a tendency to want to complete each step so that we can move on to the next step. It is hard to imagine a God who always was and always will be and who has no beginning or end. In His mind, point B does not have to follow point A, and in fact, points X, Y, and Z can happen in any order or all at the same time.

Out of chaos God can create perfection, and one of the most beautiful verses in the Bible illustrates the mind and the timing that God desires: "He has made everything beautiful in its time. He has also set eternity in the human heart; yet no one can fathom what God has done from beginning to end."[52]

In order for us to avoid the "I want it now" trap as we seek our miracle, we must exercise our faith. One of the lines I like to use is to remind myself that "faith requires feet." In other words, to demonstrate my faith I must put it into action just as Peter did when he stepped out of the boat. Putting faith into action sometimes means defying all logic.

It takes a daily struggle with oneself and a commitment to "wait upon the Lord." The Bible is rich with examples of its admonition to "wait upon the Lord," such as this example from Isaiah: "But they that wait upon the Lord shall renew their strength; they shall mount up with wings as eagles; they shall run, and not be weary;

---

[51] (KJV).
[52] Eccles. 3:11 (NIV).

and they shall walk, and not faint."[53] Another example is when the psalmist writes, "Wait on the Lord: be of good courage, and he shall strengthen thine heart: wait, I say, on the Lord."[54]

## Mistake 7: Having an "I'll Fix It Myself" Attitude

While most of us are too vain to admit it, we often are drawn into crossing over the line between working to *allow* God's miracle and trying to *make* a miracle of our own happen.

In my case I was faced with no options for a cure; nor was I given a definitive diagnosis. There is no known cure for what I have, and only limited drugs and therapies can lessen the impact. That being said, I still took out my "Mr. Fixit" mentality and tried every pill that came in a bottle to remedy the situation. While there are well-meaning practitioners of alternative medicines, there are also those poised to feed off the fears and desperation of those facing the impossible. Attempting those things that seemed rational offered a degree of hope in the face of a hopeless situation, but in my case they only stood in the way of a miracle. After trying every supplement, mineral, vitamin, and potion known to humankind, I became convicted by the Holy Spirit that I was, in a very real way, getting in God's way. God convicted me to stop doing what I was doing and let Him work. After all, if God works a miracle healing of my body at the same time I begin another supplement, who gets the credit?

As I make this point I realize that there is a fine line between doing all that we can and going too far. I have friends and family who are strong proponents of alternative and holistic health practices, and I can understand those who want to do all they can to help heal the body as naturally as possible, but in my case I let myself get in the way and went too far on the road to fixing myself.

God does not just pick out certain people for healing who

---

[53] Isaiah 40:31 (KJV).
[54] Psalm 27:14 (KJV).

have earned His "passing score" or other kinds of approval. In 2 Chronicles 16:9 we read, "For the eyes of the Lord run to and fro throughout the whole earth, to shew himself strong in the behalf of them whose heart is perfect toward him."[55] He isn't looking for someone who is perfect; He is looking for someone whose heart is perfect in Him. God is looking for those who hunger and are open-minded in the realm of the Spirit. He says, "Draw nigh [near] unto Me and I will draw nigh unto you."[56] In Psalms He says, "Delight yourself in the Lord, and he will give you the desires of your heart."[57]

## Mistake 8: Failing to Meaningfully Communicate with God

Today people's lives are so full of the junk of this world that they do not have any room for the real things of God. While modern day technology can be a blessing, it can also be a curse. Walk down almost any street, and you will see countless people walking while texting and almost lost in two different worlds at the same time. I heard it said that due to technology we're exchanging information at a greater rate than ever before, but at the same time its quality is diminishing exponentially.

I had to chuckle as I was pushing a shopping cart through a store not long ago and witnessed a teenaged boy who was walking and texting at the same time. As he walked, he ran head-on into a display unit that had been set up in the isle. He looked around just long enough to see who had witnessed the event and then immediately focused back on the device in his hands as he walked on texting.

Children and teens as well as adults are sending uncountable strings of text without hardly any real or meaningful interaction. While it is true that we are exchanging information, it's like a lake that has grown to be a mile wide but only an inch deep. On the

---

[55] (KJV).
[56] James 4:8 (KJV).
[57] Psalm 37:4 (NKJV).

surface it looks fantastic, but it's so shallow that it's meaningless and of little use to anyone.

With all of this in mind, we must ask ourselves about our level of communication with the Lord. Are we talking person-to-person daily or, are we sending strings of requests to a God who longs for a personal relationship with Him?

This new explosion in technology is harmful in many ways, not the least of which is that it is taking true interaction between people out of the equation. If people cannot learn to have meaningful communication between each other, how then can they learn to communicate with God? It is God's desire that we reach out to Him daily in love. Just as a good parent wants to hear from the heart of his or her child, our Father wants to hear from our hearts.

Jesus says in Mark, "And the cares of this world, the deceitfulness of riches, and the *lust of other things entering in, choke the Word, and it becometh unfruitful.*"[58] I am afraid that like so many other things, Satan has taken a good thing and corrupted it to weaken our relationships at all levels.

## Mistake 9: Allowing Fear to Stop You

Fear often shows up in our lives when we are at risk of losing something that is very important to us, such as health, wealth, relationships, jobs, family, loved ones, and so on. Fear reveals our deepest desire to protect those things in life that are the most important to us rather than to fully entrust them to God's loving care and to His control.

The remedy for our fear is to trust in the One who understands this most, the One who created us and knows us better than we know ourselves. Only when we trust that He is there, that we are standing in His presence with His power and His protection and

---

[58] Mark 4:19 (KJV), emphasis added.

provision, can we share the joy of the psalmist who wrote, "I sought the Lord, and he answered me; he delivered me from all my fears."[59]

## Mistake 10: Believing "Miracles Don't Apply to Me"

If we're honest, this trap of disbelief is in all of us. Even if we have evidence of a miracle in another person's life we say, "That's great for that person, but that's not going to happen to me!" That kind of defeatist attitude is an automatic win for the devil, as we lay down our weapons and surrender the battle before there is any opportunity for a win.

Remember that God loves all His children the same. While He may have issues with each of us, just as any parent would see things in his or her children that need work, God still loves each of His children the same. Romans 2:11 says it clearly: "For God does not show favoritism."[60]

We are admonished in the book of James as follows: "If any of you lacks wisdom, you should ask God, who gives generously to *all* [note: no favorites] without finding fault, and it will be given to you. But when you ask, you must believe and not doubt, because the one who doubts is like a wave of the sea, blown and tossed by the wind. That person should not expect to receive anything from the Lord."[61] The very next verse says it all: "Such a person is double-minded and unstable in all they do."[62]

## Mistake 11: Believing "God Is Upset with Me and Can't Love Me the Way I Am"

No trick of Satan is stronger than the lie that God would be upset with us and not love us as we are. It has kept more people in bondage than perhaps any other in his arsenal. This kind of thinking

---

[59] Ps. 34:4 (NIV).
[60] (NIV).
[61] James 1:5–7 (NIV).
[62] James 1:8 (NIV).

is legalism to its extreme. God's love is unconditional. That's right: He loves us without condition. *Nothing* you can do will make Him love you any less—or any more! If you're a parent, do you love your children less when they disappoint you? The answer should be no. They have disappointed you, but you don't love them based on their performance; you love them because they are your children. Why would God do anything less?

We have all had failures of faith in our walks with the Lord. This may disappoint God, but it doesn't affect His love for us. As many Christians face the biggest battles of their lives, they are bound by their pasts and focus on their own failures of faith. This is one of the devil's favorite and most powerful tools. He knows that if he can plant the seed of doubt, we'll tend it and make it grow. In fact, this is exactly the opposite of what we need. Instead of focusing on seeds of doubt, we need to nurture seeds of faith.

## Mistake 12: Believing "I Don't Know How to Unlock the Miracle God Has for Me"

God keeps His promises simple and on our level of understanding. He knows that He is beyond our comprehension. No one other than Jesus has ever fully understood the mind of God. If you think of it, would you respect and serve a God whose mind you could fully understand? If we could understand God fully, that would mean our minds were as great as His.

God's thoughts are not our thoughts and His ways are not our ways, and this is for good reason.[63] The next verse of Isaiah goes on to explain why: just "as the heavens are higher than the earth, so are [God's] ways higher than your ways and [God's] thoughts than your thoughts."[64] So when the devil tries to convince you that there is some secret order of prayers, fasting, and so on, that you just don't

---

[63] Isa. 55:8.
[64] Isa. 55:9 (NIV).

understand, remember that our God keeps things on our level. After all, He created us, and He knows our abilities and weaknesses.

Think of it this way: if your second grade child came to you feeling ill, you wouldn't tell him that you would base whether or not you helped him on his ability to solve a problem in advanced algebra, would you? God considers you His child, and if you wouldn't treat your child this way, why would your heavenly Father base His blessing on your ability to perform perfectly in your trial? Like you, God is pleased to help His children in their times of need! God keeps it simple and delights in His children.[65] In truth, God desires that we approach Him in much the same way a child approaches his or her beloved parent.

## Mistake 13: Legalism

Most dictionaries will describe legalism more or less as an "excessive conformity to the law or to a religious moral code."[66] In churches where legalism is taught, the devil can work overtime. Those who have been exposed to this dangerous way of thinking don't understand the impact this has, as they are generally made to feel unrighteous and prone to think that it is their fault that God does not answer their prayers. "After all," they tell themselves, "if I were not so undeserving, God would hear and answer my prayers and my requests for healing and/or other miracles." Again, nothing could be farther from the truth. God is a God of love, and nothing we can do will cause Him to love us more or less!

## Mistake 14: Allowing the Devil a
## Place, a Voice, and a Power

Did you ever notice that in scripture Jesus never hesitates when He comes in contact with a person possessed by a demon? He does

---

[65] Ps. 149:4.

[66] *Merriam-Webster*, s.v. "legalism," http://www.merriam-webster.com/dictionary/legalism.

not have to find a place to pray, hesitate in doubt, or ask His Father for power, does He? Instead, He speaks directly, with authority, and in the most basic way possible. He uses commands, such as, "Hold thy peace (or *be quiet!*)" and "Come out of him!"[67] And the demon instantly obeys Jesus. We as believers have the same authority and need to act the same way. The more you deny the devil a voice, the less likely he will be to interfere in your daily walk. Do what Jesus would do when the devil tries to reason with you. Quote him the scriptures; he can't argue with them. Remember we are taught in James 4:7, "Submit yourselves therefore to God. Resist the devil, and he will flee from you."[68]

## Mistake 15: Believing "I'm Not Qualified"

Colossians 1:12 gives us God's promise that we are indeed qualified for all He has for us: "and giving joyful thanks to the Father, who has qualified *you* to share in the inheritance of his holy people."[69] As believers and followers of Christ, we are qualified and equipped for all of God's blessings. We don't have to be "spiritual enough," live perfect lives, read a certain number of books, take a certain number of classes, or hear a certain number of sermons to qualify for being blessed by God, filled with the Holy Spirit, and healed! Once we have accepted Christ, we are fully qualified!

Traditional thinking has poisoned our thoughts and taught God's people that although God has already provided them with the greatest miracle of all, their salvation, they must qualify before they can receive anything else from Him. God fully equips us with all we need once we become born again, meaning we have accepted Christ as our Savior. Jesus paid the price for our salvation and therefore qualified us to receive miracles.

Isaiah 53:5 tells us that through His sacrifice He already assured

---

[67] Luke 4:35 (KJV).
[68] (KJV).
[69] (NIV), emphasis added.

us that we can receive miracles: "He was pierced for *our* transgressions [our sins], he was crushed for <u>our</u> iniquities; the punishment that brought us peace was upon him, and by his wounds *we are healed*."[70]

In Galatians 2:20 we see that we live not by our own power or ability but by Christ's. Paul reminds us that Christ sacrificed His life for all who believe in Him and trust Him as Savior. This touching verse shows the personal nature of His relationship with us: "I am crucified with Christ: nevertheless I live; yet not I, but Christ liveth in me: and the life which I now live in the flesh I live by the faith of the Son of God, who loved me, and gave himself for me."[71] It is clear that Christ lives in me and that I share in the benefits of His sacrifice—as do all of us who believe in Him.

## Mistake 16: Believing "I Don't Have the Knowledge, Faith, or Wisdom"

James 1:5–7 can be a big help in understanding the mind of God when we fear we don't have the necessary knowledge, faith, or wisdom: "If any of you lacks wisdom, you should ask God, who gives *generously* to *all* without finding fault, and it *will* be given to *you*. But when you ask, you must believe and *not doubt*, because the one who doubts is like a wave of the sea, blown and tossed by the wind. That person should *not* expect to receive anything from the Lord."[72] So the secret here is to "believe and not doubt." It could not be any clearer! If we doubt, we limit God's ability to work through us and in us. When doubt comes in, we allow it to override our faith.

Scripture clearly demonstrates that our minds are battlefields. The war is not about getting faith; it is about defeating doubt! As believers, we are not to submit to anything or anyone but God and His word. We see over and over in the life of Christ how He set the

---

[70] (NIV), emphasis added.
[71] (KJV).
[72] (NIV), emphasis added.

example and submitted to His Father in order to use His power. We need to do exactly as Christ taught and submit ourselves to God.

Paul is another whose example we can learn from and emulate. He finished the course and was willing to die for the gospel. He set aside his own doubts and weaknesses and focused on his faith in God and in His Son. He did not live on his faith alone, and he knew that his faith would be flawed by his carnal mind and doubt. Instead he showed us that he called upon faith greater than his own. He placed his faith in Christ, knowing that he would never have a failure of faith if he used Christ's perfect faith.

You cannot pray enough, study enough, or work enough to build yourself to perfect faith, so place your faith on *His* faith and trust that He will be faithful to keep His promises. Don't let your lack of faith stand in the way of getting what He desires you to have. It is His faith in us that will take us to the ultimate place we need to be and to perform the miracle that we desire.

Attitude is everything! When we know that it is God's faith living within us and working through us, we cannot be denied. Once you realize that you have working within you a far greater power than anything you could come up with on your own, you'll see that God working through you is greater than your doubt and your limitations.

You are now part of an unbeatable team. You are working not on your own but in partnership with the very God who created you! Don't be fooled by the deceiver into doubting your abilities to achieve your miracle; it is not about you! It is about the perfect partnership you have tapped into. It is *not* because of *my* ability that I can receive a miracle; it is because of *our* ability ... about *His* ability to partner with me and to accomplish all that God desires in me! After all, if we are living in a right relationship with Him, what we really want is what He really wants, and He wants His children to be blessed. When we think and act this way, He gets the praise and the glory that He and He alone deserves!

## Mistake 17: Basing Faith on Personal Life Experience

John 3:30 says. "He must increase, but I must decrease."[73] Did you ever consider that it was never God's plan for you to fail? It is Satan's plan. Why then do we buy into failure in our personal lives and in our searches for miracles? It is in great part because we substitute the doctrine of faith for a doctrine of works, and works will not get us the faith that we need. We have unknowingly learned to cope with life's challenges on our own in a dysfunctional way in order to face the unbearable frustrations of failure. Satan desires that we focus on the self in order to divert our attention away from the finished work of Christ. God's favor is upon His children, and it is inherited—*not* earned. We waste too much time and effort working to obtain what we already have, His favor and His faith. Doubt is a tool of the devil. Confidence is the key to victory.

Have you ever noticed that Paul came to the point where he caught the spirit of Christ's triumph? Paul had great success in working miracles. Just as when we go to a medical expert who provides us with insight and additional hope that helps us grow, Paul grew in knowledge and faith and took literally Jesus's promises. He gained faith from listening to Jesus, who knew far more than he knew.

We need to be more like the woman who had tried all the things the world had to offer and failed to achieve a miracle. In Luke 8:44 we see her surrender totally to her faith in Jesus's ability when she pushes her way through the crowd on her way to the one who can give her a miracle: "she came up behind him and touched the edge of his cloak, and *immediately* her bleeding stopped."[74] You'll note that she gave up trying to do it herself (she surrendered), turned to Jesus (showed faith), reached out to touch Him (put her faith into action), and *then* she received her miracle.

---

[73] (KJV).

[74] (NIV), emphasis added.

## Mistake 18: Giving Up Just Short of a Miracle

Sometimes we tell ourselves, "But I tried and nothing happened." The devil knows this and uses the power of it against us. As the Bible says, "Hope deferred makes the heart sick."[75]

God is honored when we step out in faith, especially when we don't see actions or His response immediately. Look at the example of the children of Israel in Joshua 6:2–20 as they march around Jericho. I am sure that as they march around the first time without results, they begin to wonder, "Why didn't it happen?" And when they march a second, third, fourth, fifth, and sixth time, the devil must really be going to work. "See, no results," he might tell them. "Your faith doesn't work." Or maybe he says, "There is no God" or "You're doing it wrong" or "God doesn't hear you" or "Your God is too busy to hear your petty request," and so on. Does this sound familiar? That's the way Satan works. But faith is just that: believing that God will do the work necessary at the time that is best.

If we read the instructions they are given, we'll see that the instructions don't tell them to march one or two times. They say to march for six days and on the seventh day to have "seven priests" bearing "seven trumpets of rams' horns … compass the city seven times" and then blow the trumpets. Then the people are to shout a "great shout."[76] This process takes what must seem to be forever, but the believers do as they are told (not as they feel), and they see God's miracle occur: the walls crumble, and they take the city! Just as they press forward in the face of an apparent lack of results and the scorns of nonbelievers, we too must say that old line: "God said it, I believe it, and that settles it!" Faith does not back up; it moves forward, or it is not faith!

## Mistake 19: Shutting Out Other Believers

When faced with challenges, believers demonstrate a wide range

---

[75] Prov. 13:12 (NIV).
[76] Joshua 6:3.

of responses. Some people boldly admit their struggle and reach out to others, while there are others who, for whatever reason, choose to suffer in silence.

In James 5:14–15 we see clear evidence that God intends for us to pray for each other, especially the body of believers (His church): "Is any sick among you? Let him call for the elders of the church; and let them pray over him, anointing him with oil in the name of the Lord: And the prayer of faith shall save the sick, and the Lord shall raise him up."[77]

One of the mistakes I quickly reversed on my journey to a miracle was shutting out others around me because of shame. I cannot tell you how much I was touched and blessed on my journey when I finally realized that I was not alone; in fact, I was stunned by all the believers who loved me and actually desired to pray for me! As I opened the mailbox or read emails each day I became more and more blessed: God was showing me all of those around me who were praying for me and who were in agreement with me as I asked Him for a miracle.

There is indeed great power in being around others who believe; it is no wonder that God encourages us to not give up "meeting together, as some are in the habit of doing, [and] encouraging one another—and all the more as you see the Day approaching."[78]

## Mistake 20: Prayer Mistakes

We live in a society of instant gratification, which has tainted our prayer lives. Imagine if you could go directly to the pharmacy without first seeking a physician's diagnosis or prescription. Through no wrongful intent, each of us has developed a faulty prayer routine that does exactly this. I like to say it this way: we've stopped treating God as the Great Physician and started using Him as our Spiritual Pharmacist.

---

[77] (KJV).
[78] Heb. 10:25 (NIV).

In real life you don't go directly to your pharmacy, diagnose yourself, and then tell the pharmacist what you think will solve your problem or make you feel better. That would be foolishness, since you are not a doctor. How do *I* know what I need or what the cause is for my sickness? Yet without first going to our heavenly Father and seeking His advice, we routinely begin our prayers with our own desires: "God, grant me a new job," we might pray, or perhaps we ask for more money, physical healing, and so on. What if your desire is not in your best interest, not in God's plan, or would rob you of an even greater blessing?

Instead of unrolling your list of "God, please grant me" requests, try this: "Lord, I ask you for nothing today; instead, please show me what's on your heart for me today." Then listen for His answer, for as long as it takes. You'll be amazed when you stop asking and begin listening. True communication is two ways, and no one can talk and listen at the same time.

## Mistake 21: Seeking God's Answers on *Our* Time Frame

Think of Mary and Martha's prayer as they watched Lazarus getting sicker and sicker and then approaching death. Had their prayers been answered in their way, Jesus would have shown up and healed Lazarus (and yes, that would have been a miracle), but by waiting until Lazarus had been dead for three days and *then* raising him from the dead, Jesus gave them what they desired, a healthy Lazarus, in a fashion that made it one of the greatest miracles recorded in the Bible *and* a preview of Christ's own resurrection from the grave! We each must learn to wait for God and to trust His plan for each of us. Think about it this way, Jesus did not show up three days late, He showed up right on time!

## Mistake 22: The Doubting Thomas Syndrome

The doubting Thomas syndrome entails saying something like, "Lord, I will only believe in you if you prove yourself through providing me with my miracle." One of my favorite verses of scripture is Romans 4:17. If we study that verse in context, we see that Abraham was not called "father" because he got God's attention and favor by the way he lived, but because he trusted God. Abraham was named father before he became a father, because he dared to trust God. When all was hopeless, Abraham believed anyway. He chose to live by what God said *He* would do through him. His faith in God was well placed, and Abraham became the father of a multitude of peoples.

## Mistake 23: Allowing Known Sin to Remain

One of the most dangerous things a believer can do is to rationalize or create personal justifications for sin. The Bible clearly points out the danger of allowing a little sin to remain in a believer's life: "A little yeast works through the whole batch of dough."[79] God cannot tolerate *any* sin, and as we seek to grow closer to Him, neither should we. God is spotless: "Your eyes are too pure to look on evil; you cannot tolerate wrong."[80] You may try to justify your sin by saying, "But hasn't Jesus paid for all my sins?" Or you might ask, "After all, why should I be concerned about sin when God loves me and has already sacrificed His Son for my sin?" God never views sin as small. To Him, sin is sin! In our natural lives we try to grade sin on a curve; we justify that our sin, the one we won't give up, isn't really all that bad. After all, we might say, "People commit far greater sins than my tiny infraction." Ask any alcoholic to define what an alcoholic is, and he or she will almost always say, "An alcoholic is someone who drinks more than I do." Before you laugh at that, try this: replace the word *alcoholic* with that thing that God wants out of your life, and then repeat the exercise. Again, God does not grade sin on a curve. Sin is sin to God.

Because of only one sin, Adam and Eve were exiled from the

---

[79] Gal. 5:9 (NIV).
[80] Hab. 1:13 (NIV).

Garden of Eden, and all of creation was corrupted. Because of other sins that people justified, God brought a flood upon the earth's inhabitants in the days of Noah. Because of sexual sins, God rained down fire on Sodom and Gomorrah. Similarly, it was sin that kept the children of Israel in the wilderness for forty years.

Like Adam and Eve, we think we can disobey a little and not be overcome by it. Whenever we sin, we place something between God and us. His Spirit inside you is grieved, and if you are honest, you will admit that you know this. When we sin, we are choosing at that instant to live independently of the Lord's will for us. No, God does not hate you for this. He still loves you, but it saddens Him and separates us from Him. We're warned in Ephesians 4:30 not to "grieve the Holy Spirit of God, whereby ye are sealed unto the day of redemption."[81]

Sin does not affect God's eternal relationships with us because those relationships were settled when we trusted in Christ's payment for our sins and accepted Him as Savior.

Because of your faith in Jesus alone, you are totally forgiven. Your relationship with God is secure. But sin affects your fellowship with God. You might think of fellowship as your day-to-day walk with the Lord. How easy is it to walk next to a friend when you know you have something wrong between you? You talk less and less, become distant, and grow apart.

Sin affects our communication with God and our daily fellowship with Him. Sin hinders us from doing the things Christ wants us to be doing.

Confessing sin is agreeing with God. God knows that you've sinned or that you're allowing sin in your life. Honesty is the best policy: "If we confess our sins, he is faithful and just and will forgive us our sins and purify us from all unrighteousness."[82] Confession does not mean begging God for forgiveness. Christ already paid

---

[81] (KJV).
[82] 1 John 1:9 (NIV).

42

the penalty for all our sins, and God's forgiveness is available automatically when we confess our sin to Him.

Repentance is the next natural step. Repentance simply means to change directions, attitudes, and actions concerning your sin. You agree with God that you were wrong and that you do not want to continue to commit your sin any longer or give it a place in your life.

## But What If I Still Feel Guilty?

The devil loves to whisper guilty thoughts in our ears and tempt us to sin again. Remember that temptation is not a sin and that what God forgives is forgotten: "as far as the east is from the west, so far has he removed our transgressions from us."[83] Everyone is tempted! Even Jesus was tempted, but He didn't give in to His temptations. Just because He was tempted did not mean He sinned. If you are being tempted, don't beat yourself up. God understands. Decide not to dwell on tempting thoughts, and ask God for the strength to avoid the sin. A great verse to keep at hand is Romans 8:1, which says, "Therefore, there is now no condemnation for those who are in Christ Jesus."[84]

[83] Ps. 103:12 (KJV).
[84] (NIV).

# CHAPTER 4

# DOING ALL THE RIGHT THINGS FOR THE RIGHT REASONS

HOW CAN WE TELL IF we're doing the right thing? In the previous chapter we discussed all the mistakes we can make when facing the seemingly impossible. In this chapter I'll attempt to explore the tools we have at our disposal as we seek God's supernatural assistance.

## Action 1: Put the Enemy in His Place

Scripture clearly teaches that the devil is a liar and the father of all lies, so we need to put him in his place.[85] He wants nothing less than the destruction of believers and is a master of weaving himself inconspicuously into life's challenges. Did you ever notice that he doesn't appear to Eve in the Garden of Eden looking like the stereotypical devil? No red suit, no pointy tail, no horns, no pitchfork. Instead he appears as a normal part of her environment: "Now the serpent was more subtle than any beast of the field which the Lord God had made."[86] He uses the same tactic today, appearing in a myriad of disguises and still planting doubt.

When the father of all lies enters your garden, it's time to put

---

[85] John 8:44.
[86] Gen. 3:1 (KJV).

him in his place. Do what Jesus does when Satan attempts to trick Him: use the most powerful tool of all, the very word of God. The Bible demonstrates that Jesus often puts Satan in his place, reminding us that Satan has no truth in him.[87] The word *devil* literally means "adversary" or "accuser," which is his true character. That is not what he wants us to believe about him.

As believers we must continually remind ourselves that Satan is our true enemy and that he constantly seeks to undermine us in everything we do, especially when we do it for Christ. Scripture reminds us of his true intent, describing him as being like a lion seeking those to devour.[88]

## Action 2: Remember God's Promises

Remember God's promises. Jesus says in Matthew 10:8 that we have received the power to "heal the sick, cleanse the lepers, raise the dead, [and] cast out devils" and that we are to share this with others. "Freely ye have received, freely give."[89]

## Action 3: Put Your Oxygen Mask on First

When you are faced with a challenge greater than your ability, it is crucial to admit you need help. If you need help and feel comfortable admitting this to others, then good for you! If not, you can be your own worst enemy. Being a take-charge, type A personality, who is never comfortable being on the receiving end of compassion, I can admit that this has been a big struggle for me.

When counseling others, I commonly see hurting people unwilling to admit they are in great emotional pain. They try to cope with all of life's issues as if they were not hurting. When faced with someone like this, I will give the following illustration: Imagine that you have been badly hurt in an automobile accident and have

---

[87] John 8:44.
[88] 1 Pet. 5:8.
[89] (KJV).

been taken to the emergency room. Once there, you realize that the person in the other car, who was also injured, is the doctor who must now help you. He comes into your room bloodied and severely injured and prepares to work on you. If this happened, what would you say? Naturally, you'd say, "How can he help me in the condition he's in? Get me someone else!" While this sounds ridiculous, this doctor's actions reflect exactly what we do when we are hurting and attempting to simply go on with life. It's okay to admit you are hurting and to reach out for help.

I fly a lot, and on a recent flight from Florida I heard the usual cascade of announcements from the flight attendant about how to fasten your seatbelt, and so on. One announcement made me think of a truth that applies to each of us when faced with a crisis: we cannot help others until we first take care of ourselves. Maybe you have noticed the strange announcement that goes something like "in the unlikely event that the aircraft depressurizes, oxygen masks will drop from the ceiling. Adults are to place their masks on first before securing them on their children." To many, this might seem callous; after all, what parent wouldn't help his or her child first? As a pilot myself, I know that this announcement makes good sense. In the event that the cabin loses pressure, you only have a few seconds before you'll pass out from a lack of oxygen. If you attempt to help others first, you might end up helping no one at all.

Such is the case with healing. Before helping others, you have to take care of yourself. In so doing, you'll be better equipped to help others in their time of need. In fact, by learning about healing and seeking God's direction, you'll be stronger and better equipped to help others. Perhaps more importantly, you'll be stronger yourself!

## Action 4: Keep Moving Forward Whenever Possible

A sure way to begin to decline is to stop growing. In Matthew 5:6, Jesus says, "Blessed *are* those who hunger and thirst for righteousness, For they shall be filled."[90] If we want to see God be God, we cannot sit down in the middle of our crisis and wait for something good to happen. Chances are that just the opposite will occur; instead of growing, we will begin the gradual slide toward decay.

One thing I learned early on in my search was that just like every other tool, the Internet can be either a valuable resource or something the enemy can use to bring us down. I often advise people to limit their use of the Internet, especially discussion rooms that seem like a rich resource for those going through a trial. Well-intentioned people enter medical discussion pages and then soon begin using them to vent their frustrations and post every possible negative consequence of a disease, drug, or treatment. I lost plenty of sleep to scouring the Internet for answers and support only to find myself deeply depressed and wallowing in despair after reading countless stories about hopeless situations and despairing people. Although they should, people who are coping well with a disease rarely post much on Internet sites like these.

If I could give you some direction about discussion sites on the Internet, I would say use them sparingly and only use well-known sites hosted and moderated by professional medical staff. Using sites that are not moderated leads only to unsubstantiated anecdotal observations, which the devil loves to use against us to inspire fear. Many of these horrible stories are only partially based on fact; most likely, frustration has led to an exaggeration of a person's reality.

## Action 5: Pray for Others

The words *effectual* and *fervent* in James 5:16 both relate to energy. In other words, you really add power and show God the depth of your love when you pour your heart out to Him for a miracle for others.

James 5:16 reminds us to "pray one for another, that ye may be

---

[90] Matthew 5:6 (NKJV)

healed. The effectual fervent prayer of a righteous man availeth [or accomplishes] much."[91] God clearly expects us to pray unselfishly for others. Just as we are encouraged to present our personal needs to Him, God is clearly pleased when we set aside our own needs and take time to lift up another's needs before our own. God brings total restoration to Job when Job sets aside his self-interest and begins to intercede for his friends. In the midst of Job's prayerful intercession for his friends, God actually gives him what he needs: "After Job had prayed for his friends, the Lord restored his fortunes and gave him twice as much as he had before."[92] Note that God not only returns all that Job has lost, including his health, family, and possessions, but He also gives him twice as much as he had before. Praying for others is clearly a turning point in Job's search for his own miracle.

When we are in the middle of a storm or a battle, we can easily sink into an "every man for himself" mentality. We have all heard of those few heroes who, while facing imminent danger, sacrifice their very lives for the welfare of others, some who they don't even know. This same sense of sacrifice can add real power to our prayers and petitions to our heavenly Father.

While writing this section, I have been reminded of something that we are all most likely guilty of: praying for others that *we* love and care about instead of praying for *all* people who need our prayers. Each time we pray, we should ask God to help us remember all of those we should be praying for, not just those we frequently remember.

Prayer is asking in faith, not asking "in just the right way." Since God is no respecter of persons, He shows no favoritism, so it really does not make a difference if the prayer and the faith behind it are coming from a great leader of the church, a tiny child, a young father, an elderly mother, a spouse, or a friend.[93] The power of prayer

---

[91] (KJV).

[92] Job 42:10 (NIV).

[93] Rom. 2:11.

is based upon the *promises* of God, not on the power of our faith alone.

## Action 6: Look for Evidence of Miracles

A friend of mine once reminded me that Satan loves when we *speak into existence* our negative thoughts. Entire books have been written on the power of the tongue, and scripture is rich with verses about our need to control it. Proverbs 18:21 reminds us that "death and life are in the power of the tongue: and they that love it shall eat the fruit thereof."[94]

God desires that our faith be real and shown by our actions, including what comes out of our mouths. Isaiah 55:11 offers us a powerful lesson on the words we speak about God's promises: "So is my word that goes out from my mouth: It will not return to me empty, but will accomplish what I desire and achieve the purpose for which I sent it."[95]

Satan loves to point out the supposed evidence that God is not working in our lives, but remember that he is a liar and the father of liars.[96] He naturally will try to destroy your hope by presenting what appears to be God's lack of action of your behalf. Remember that Satan tried to challenge Christ's mind when He was at His weakest during a forty-day fast. Why would he not do the same to us during our times of trial? Jesus showed us what to do when approached in this manner: we are to use the word of God instead of listening to the one who wants nothing short of our eternal destruction.

In short, look constantly for the evidence that God is working in your situation, and speak out about what you see Him doing. In so doing, you'll strengthen your faith rather than weaken it.

---

[94] (KJV).
[95] (NIV).
[96] John 8:44.

## Action 7: Forgiveness

Please read this in its entirety: One of the most powerful tools a Christian has is the power of forgiveness, we must start by forgiving ourselves. Whether we realize it or not, people are usually unwilling to forgive themselves and to recognize that God's sacrifice of Christ was all about forgiveness. God promises, "As far as the east is from the west, so far hath he removed our transgressions from us."[97]

He has already cleansed us to do His work and so He can live in and through us: "How much more, then, will the blood of Christ, who through the eternal Spirit offered himself unblemished to God, cleanse our consciences from acts that lead to death, so that we may serve the living God!"[98] God cleanses us for His service so that we are not left with the shame and guilt of our sin but are instead alive through our victory in Christ. The beginning of self-forgiveness is making sure that our guilt of sin is gone forever!

Next, we must each forgive all of those who need forgiveness—not *some*, but *all*. Think of Christ's last act of forgiving others as He hung on the cross. He asked His heavenly Father to forgive the very men who had just nailed Him to the cross. The key is in what He said next: "they know not what they do." Even those who don't seem to deserve it require our forgiveness, if for no other reason than because they don't realize what it is they are doing.

The third person we may have to forgive, if we have bitterness toward Him, is God Himself. While the thought may seem foreign to you, there are those who blame God because one of their children died, because of an unfaithful spouse, because they have been sick and God has not answered their request for healing, because they lost a job or don't have enough money to pay their mortgage, and so on. Consciously or subconsciously, they place the blame on God. Forgiving God is critical, as being unforgiving is an obstacle to seeking a miracle from God. This may take some serious

---

[97] Ps. 103:12 (KJV).
[98] Heb. 9:14 (NIV).

soul-searching, but you must ask yourself, "Am I blaming God for my situation?"

Next you'll need to forgive those closest to you. Yes, you even must forgive your parents, children, spouse, and relatives. All issues, hurts, wounds, and past injuries must be dealt with.

And finally, you must forgive all others. Trust me on this one: God will reveal a long list if you genuinely ask Him to. Matthew 5:23–24 gives powerful witness to this fact: "Therefore, if you are offering your gift at the altar [approaching God] and there remember that your brother or sister has something against you; leave your gift there in front of the altar. First go and be reconciled to them; then come and offer your gift."[99] Simply stated, don't approach God when you have an issue involving a lack of forgiveness; that needs to be dealt with first. This can often be very difficult, especially if your resentment seems justified. The person may have done a terrible thing to you. But if you want to see miracles in your life, it is absolutely imperative that you forgive that person, just as God, through Christ, has forgiven you unconditionally!

This section is extremely important, which is why I started by asking you to read the whole thing. The enemy has no stronger weapon against us than blocking forgiveness, and we have no more powerful weapon against him than true forgiveness!

[99] (NIV).

# CHAPTER 5

# GOD HEALS ALL BELIEVERS WHO ASK HIM, AND THE ANSWER IS NEVER NO!

YOU MIGHT FIND THE TITLE of this chapter hard to believe. How could anyone say that God heals all believers who ask Him and that the answer is never no? A truth I learned on this journey toward finding my own miracle is that God always answers believers' requests for miracles and always grants them a miracle, but He does so in His way.

God answers in His way—not in our way, in our time, or even in our manner. I felt strongly led to write this book after watching countless preachers and others with the "gift of healing" who only facilitated instantaneous miracles. But what about all of those who do not instantly receive healing? Doesn't God care about them? Doesn't God hear their requests? The answer will be clear later in this chapter.

An examination of Jesus's healing miracles during His time on earth reveals facts about how He healed and whom He healed. Scripture shows us that He healed by the word, by the faith of the person involved, to restore life, to deliver people from demons, through the faith of others, through the faith of the persistent, and to reveal God to others.

I have identified five different ways in which God answers believers' requests for miracles which I will discuss in detail later in this chapter. Note that I specify *believers* for a specific reason. God can work miracles in the lives of nonbelievers; however, not all of these five apply to the nonbeliever since a nonbeliever's salvation and eternal security are in question. (The term *believers* here refers to those people who trust in Jesus's sacrifice on the cross for their sins and have accepted Him as their Lord and Savior).

But does God really still heal the sick? In one word, the answer is yes. We can see God doing it in the Old Testament and Jesus doing it in the New Testament. Remember that "The God of yesterday is the God of today" and "Jesus Christ is the same yesterday and today and forever."[100] Let me say it again: God always heals believers. God answers all their requests for healing, and He does it in one of five different ways.

Before we look at the five ways, let's look at what a true miracle really is: The term *miracle* has lost much of its meaning in our day. The reason for this is not that we see miracles occurring so often that we are desensitized to their meaning. It's because our speech has evolved in such a way that if I got to work on time this morning, it was a "miracle."

The biblical definition of a miracle, on the other hand, is another thing all together. Not everything hard to believe can be quantified as a "miracle" according to scriptural standards. Miracles are those acts that supersede natural laws and that only God can perform. This is worth restating: a miracle is an act that *only* God can perform, and it supersedes natural law.

A miracle reveals that the power behind it is *not limited to the laws of matter or nature.*

It's very interesting that a common word for *miracle* in the New Testament can also be translated *sign*. A miracle is a sign that God

---

[100] Heb. 13:8 (NIV).

uses to point to Himself in the same way we follow signs to find a hospital, police station, or airport.

Merriam-Webster's Dictionary defines a miracle as "an extraordinary event manifesting divine intervention in human affairs."[101]

Jesus's miracles in the Bible have common qualities:

- God doesn't use miracles casually.
- God doesn't like to have to prove Himself to us by using miracles to make us believe. Remember doubting Thomas?
- He expects us to show our faith and to do *our* part (the possible) in order for Him to do *His* part (the impossible or supernatural).

Now, let's explore the five ways that God performs miracles of healing for His children.

## 1: God Heals through Natural Processes

The first way God heals is through natural processes. He put natural healing in place at the time of His creation. It *is* something that God provides us with to accomplish healing.

There are countless ways God heals through natural processes. When we break bones, our bodies mend themselves. God does that! I have often said that if doctors practiced total honestly, they would have a sign in their waiting rooms that reads "100 percent of my patients will die!" While we benefit greatly from the skill, knowledge, and training of physicians, I must point out that no physician has ever healed a single cell in even one body. They are only wise tools that God uses to facilitate His healing in each of us.

If I poke a hole in a balloon filled with water, eventually all the water will leak out; the balloon will not heal. However, because an

---

[101] *The Merriam-Webster Online Dictionary*, s.v. "miracle," http://www.merriam-webster.com/dictionary/miracle.

all-knowing God created us, He also created in each of us the ability to heal. Poke a similar hole in my skin, and blood will leak out, but unlike the balloon, the wound quickly stops bleeding.

So we see that healing is possible because of the very way God created us. If you thank your doctor (and you should), you should also thank your Father, our Great Physician, as well.

We should never discount healing as *simply* natural healing; it is healing that occurs because of the great wisdom and design of an almighty God. The way He created our bodies to recover is amazing.

## 2: God Heals *through* Doctors and *through* Medicines

Now let's give thanks to those who practice medicine and assist God in healing. As the Bible says, "Every good and perfect gift is from above, coming down from the Father of the heavenly lights, who does not change like shifting shadows."[102] Anyone who has had surgery or medical care knows this and knows that medical care and surgery can help bring about healing.

God heals through doctors and through medicines, surgeries, therapies, treatments, and so on. But the key here is that *they* don't do the healing; God does!

Using doctors does not show a lack of faith. Remember that God created doctors, and He can use them in caring for our earthly bodies. It is also commonly believed that Luke was a physician. Paul calls him "the beloved physician," and undoubtedly one reason for his ongoing association with Paul was Paul's need for frequent medical care.[103] Paul speaks of a medical problem that he calls a "thorn in the flesh," for example, and he also speaks about his "infirmities."[104]

In Jesus's day, He endorsed the medical practices of the time, such as the use of oil and wine. We see Jesus praise the Good

---

[102] James 1:17 (NIV).
[103] Col. 4:14.
[104] 2 Cor. 12:7, 9 (KJV).

Samaritan for acting like a physician, and He tells His disciples to go and do the same.

## 3: God Performs Supernatural Healings

Supernatural healing is the type of miracle or "miraculous healing" that many of us think of and desire when we ask God to heal us. Quite honestly, it's the healing that I most often request of God when I pray for those in need.

To understand this type of healing, it is important to understand the definition of *supernatural*. When something is deemed supernatural, it is being attributed to some force beyond scientific understanding and the laws of nature. This type of miracle is the most easily seen and recognized. One of the many reasons why thousands flocked to see Jesus when He walked the earth was that He regularly performed supernatural healings. I truly believe that a sudden miracle like this is usually not a matter of faith on the part of the one healed; it's a matter of the glory to God. The choice is up to Him!

Whenever I pray for a sick person, I always pray for this kind of healing, but if God chooses one of the other four types, I've learned to trust Him with that. We'll look at supernatural healings in more detail later in this book.

## 4: "Greater Work" or "Inner Healing" Miracles

Greater work miracles or inner healing miracles are also often referred to as "process healings." This is the type of healing I received, as I'll expand upon later. Unlike instantaneous miracles, a process miracle is a process of healing whereby God delivers *more* than just the healing we desire for *our* purposes; He works through the situation for *His* purpose. Sometimes God wants to do a greater work in us and allows us to go through a process and yes, even to struggle if that is what's needed to accomplish the change He desires in us.

We often forget that even this process is also found in scripture.

When Paul prays to be delivered from the thorn in the flesh, God says, "My grace is sufficient for you, for *my power is made perfect in weakness* ... Therefore I will boast all the more gladly about my weaknesses, so that Christ's power may rest on me."[105] You'll note that in process healing His power is "made perfect" in our weakness! Many would say that the entire book of Job fits into this category of healing.

Sometimes God receives more glory through our responses to suffering than from His supernatural healings—and we must accept that. Some of the most beautiful people I've ever met are those who have suffered much—and suffered well, as in the example we learn from reading about Job's journey.

## 5: Ultimate Healing

Ultimate healing only applies to believers who have accepted Christ.

While we are in our earthly bodies, we do not appreciate ultimate healing as we should. We all will, however, one day be thankful for it.

Ultimate healing is when God brings a person home to be with Him. This is not a refusal to heal; it is the ultimate healing! With ultimate healing, there is no more sickness, no more pain, and no more sorrows; instead, we rejoice forever with the Lord.

All believers hope to receive an ultimate healing, and we should, especially if we consider that even a miraculous healing of our bodies is really only temporary. Have you ever considered that all the people Christ healed in His ministry ultimately died one day? Not even one person who Jesus healed as He walked on this earth is alive today!

One day each of our bodies will give out, and how glorious it will be when that happens to never have to be concerned again with our physical flesh. We will not have to endure any more doctors, hospitals, medications, surgeries, treatments, procedures, or suffering.

---

[105] 2 Cor. 12:9 (NIV), emphasis added.

*Robert W. Littke, Ph.D.*

## Are You Still in Doubt?

If after reading this section you still question whether God really grants healings freely to those who come to Him, do a small study of the miracles that Jesus did in His day, and focus on His success rate. You'll quickly see that He had a 100 percent success rate and that He healed *all*, not just some, who came to Him. Also take note that each healing was unique.

- In Matthew 4:23–24, Jesus went about Galilee teaching in the synagogues and healing *all*.
- In Mark 1:33–34, as the whole town came to Him, He healed *all* their illnesses.
- In Matthew 8:16, in Capernaum, Jesus healed *all* who were sick.
- In Mark 6:56, they laid the sick in the streets, and *as many as touched Him* were made whole.
- In Matthew 9:35, the Bible says, "Jesus went through all the towns and villages, teaching in their synagogues, proclaiming the good news of the kingdom and healing *every* disease and sickness."[106]
- Matthew 12:15 says, "Great multitudes followed Him and He healed them *all*."[107]
- Luke 5:15 says, "Great multitudes came together to hear, and to be healed by him of their infirmities."[108]
- Matthew 14:14 says He healed them *all*.
- Luke 9:11 says that He "healed them that had need of healing."[109]

You may struggle with the fact that Jesus healed them *all*,

---

[106] (NIV), emphasis added.
[107] (KJV), emphasis added.
[108] (KJV).
[109] (KJV).

believers and nonbelievers, saints and sinners, alike. After I spent considerable study and personal reflection on this fact, the Holy Spirit convicted my heart that my struggle was evidence of my own personal bent toward legalism. The reason I struggled had to do with my tendency to judge others, leading to my own prejudice toward those who are not like me—those who have not yet come to accept Christ.

If Jesus healed all, believers and nonbelievers, He did so for the right reason. He was not endorsing their lack of Him but giving them evidence of His might and His glory so that they too would be drawn to Him and grow in their desire for Him as their Lord and Savior.

CHAPTER 6

# HIS PROMISES ARE
# FOR US TODAY

G OD DOES NOT CHANGE. As the Bible says, "Jesus Christ [is]
the same yesterday, and today, and forever."[110]

God's word likewise does not change; it is alive: "For
the word of God is alive and active. Sharper than any double-edged
sword, it penetrates even to dividing soul and spirit, joints and
marrow; it judges the thoughts and attitudes of the heart."[111] This
certainty is quite different from today's ever-changing thoughts and
opinions. With God, there is no sense of time: what He was He
is. We wouldn't think of wasting our time reading last month's
newspaper, because it is already out-of-date. God's word, however,
is never a thing of the past, nor is it outdated or dead. God cannot
even speak in the past tense. He is ever living. What He said then
He is saying now; what He commanded then He is commanding
now; what He hated then He still hates, and what He says He loved,
He still loves.

Scripture teaches us that God does not change. Unlike the world
we now live in, where opinions seem to rule the media and change
with every wind, His word does not change. God's mind does not

---

[110] Heb. 13:8 (KJV), emphasis added.
[111] Heb. 4:12 (NIV).

change, and He does not base His actions on the ever-changing opinions of human beings. Heb. 13:8 states it simply: "Jesus Christ [is] the same yesterday, and today, and *forever.*"[112] This was just as true when Jesus walked on earth, performing miracles, as it is today.

Repeatedly in the Old and New Testaments we see the same reminder that God does not change. In Malachi 3:6 we read, "For I am the Lord, I change not."[113] Isaiah 40:8 says, "The grass withereth, the flower fadeth: but the word of our God shall stand for ever."[114] In James 1:17 we read, "Every good and perfect gift is from above, coming down from the Father of the heavenly lights, who does not change like shifting shadows."[115] And in Numbers 23:19 we see that "God is not human, that he should lie, not a human being, that he should change his mind."[116]

One mistake we all are tempted to make is to think that if God does not change, then He must always react in the same way. In reality, this thought process puts God in a box and limits His reaction to our individual situations. I was guilty of this, as I would read about a miracle, attempt to duplicate the request of the person in the Bible who had received it, and then expect God to grant me a miracle in a similar fashion. When we read that God does not change, this is referring to His character and His nature, not that He will react the same way in every situation.

When God changes His mind, we view it only from a human perspective. God knows all things and has always known the ultimate plan He would carry out, even if it meant changing His reaction. We see examples of this in the Bible, such as when Jonah reaches the people of Nineveh and they repent. God relents from the destruction that was to come upon all the inhabitants. The lesson to be learned here is not that we should attempt to know exactly

---

[112] (KJV), emphasis added.
[113] (KJV).
[114] (KJV).
[115] (NIV).
[116] (NIV).

how God will react in response to our requests, but rather that we should be faithful to His word and trust Him. He alone knows what is best in our individual situations and personalizes His response to our individual needs. Just as the title of this book implies, we must search for our *own* miracles that are unique to our needs and to God's plan for each of us as individuals. Don't forget: God created only one person in the universe that is uniquely you, and He loves you in a way that He loves no one else. You are special to Him, and He has a special plan for your life that is unique to you!

## But Am I Asking for the Impossible?

In Matthew 19:26, Jesus tells His disciples, "With men this is impossible, but with God all things are possible."[117] I often recall a line that I shared with my Sunday school class many years ago: "The most impossible thing you can imagine isn't even a challenge to God!" If, for example, scientists learned that our moon was slowly coming closer and closer and would soon enter our atmosphere and destroy the earth, we would no doubt put our total earthly resources toward working on a way to prevent this catastrophic event from happening. Scientists from every nation would devote their total efforts to developing an action plan. We might attempt to send rockets armed with nuclear bombs to the moon to shock it back into place. Surely, even with all of humankind's efforts, we could not budge the moon one inch farther away from earth, yet the God of the Universe, who exceeds all natural laws, could simply speak the words "be ye removed" and cast it across the universe!

Just like those scientists, we too often try to do that which is impossible for us, and we compound the problem by not turning to the God who is capable of doing the impossible!

At the End of Our Weakness Is God's Strength

Remember when I was talking about how God sometimes allows us to go through a process instead of granting us an instantaneous

---

[117] (NIV).

miracle? Don't take this lightly or as anything less than it is—a special miracle with an added blessing! In 2 Corinthians 12:9 God says, "My grace is sufficient for you, for my power is made perfect in weakness. Therefore I will boast all the more gladly about my weaknesses, so that Christ's *power may rest on me.*"[118]

People in our society have been taught to solve problems, which is usually a good thing, until we reach our limits and keep trying to solve the impossible. Men in particular are guilty of this; I see it all the time when counseling couples. The woman is frustrated that when she wishes to talk about something deeply troubling her, her spouse doesn't listen to her heart's concern. Instead he immediately begins to offer solutions to solve the dilemma.

God respects us and expects us to do our part in surviving life's trials and in seeking miracles. God wants us to put our faith into action, but He knows our limits! After all, it was God who created us, and He knows the limits of His creation. It is during times of weakness that we can get closest to God, and that is His desire: "Draw nigh [come close] to God, and he will draw nigh to you."[119]

When we face the impossible, God desires us to draw close to Him and to get out of the way so that His grace and power can be perfected in us.

There can actually be value in recognition of our own limitations or weakness. To be weak is to be helpless because we have died to our own ambitions, desires, and abilities. When we die to the self in this way, the strength of God will be perfected in us. It is then that we will gain His strength. God desires to give His children what they want, and like any good father, He desires to see His children blessed. In fact, it is through the blessings of His children and through His Son that He is blessed: "And I will do whatever you ask in my name, so that the Son may bring glory to the Father."[120]

---

[118] (NIV), emphasis added.
[119] James 4:8 (KJV).
[120] John 14:13 (NIV).

# CHAPTER 7

# CONTROL YOUR THOUGHTS

ONTROL YOUR THOUGHTS, OR THEY'LL control you: "For as he thinks in his heart, so is he."[121]

I recall the words of one of my professors long ago who said, "Change the way you look at things, and the things you look at change." As a psychologist, I was always taught a simple truth: first you think, and then you become what you've been thinking.

One truth I was reminded of many times on my journey to a miracle was that if you don't talk out your emotions, you swallow them and they manifest themselves in your body. This applies to talking to those around you, and it especially applies to being honest with God.

Being raised in a church home and influenced by various teachings and traditions means we can perceive a very judgmental God whom we must always approach with a guarded sense of honor, respect, and reverence. While there is value in our reverent respect for God, He is also the one who created us, and just as our earthly fathers would desire, He wants us to be totally honest with Him—and yes, *totally* means *totally*.

Allow me for a moment to challenge the way you think you should talk to God. While you've probably never thought of it this

---

[121] Proverbs 23:7 (NKJV).

way, it's okay to *unload* on God. Yes, you heard me right! He's a big God, and He already knows what's on your mind. He is waiting for you to trust Him enough to tell Him what you are struggling with. Don't worry; He can take it, and He won't love you any less for unloading on Him.

Think of it this way: if one of your children has a fit in the middle of a store, would it cause you to love your child less? Of course not. As a mature adult, you would stand with your child. Even if you were disappointed, your child's "venting" would not make you lose faith in him or her. God can likewise handle your temper tantrums, and He won't love you any less if you'll just be honest with Him.

Proverbs 29:18 says, "Where there is no vision, the people perish: but he that keepeth the law, happy is he."[122] There are two categories of people identified within this verse. The first don't have vision, and they perish. The second mentally see God's word as reality and as truth. This actually brings them pleasure! They decide to have a vision and to proceed with a purpose.

Many of us were taught that an idle mind is the devil's workshop. There is a lot of truth in that simple statement, and it is as true today as it was when we were younger. Satan is still looking for an opportunity to mess with our minds. Ephesians 6:12 reminds us that there is a war going on, and it is spiritual in nature. Satan's greatest desire is to control your thought life. He knows that if he can plant seeds of fear, distrust, and confusion in our minds, he can control us.

We see an example of the way God desires us to think in Ephesians 4:17–23, which gives us instructions for Christian living:

> So I tell you this, and insist on it in the Lord, that you must no longer live as the Gentiles do, in the futility of their thinking. [In other words, don't think like the worldly.] They are darkened in their

---

[122] (KJV).

understanding and separated from the life of God because of the ignorance that is in them due to the hardening of their hearts. Having lost all sensitivity, they have given themselves over to sensuality so as to indulge in every kind of impurity, and they are full of greed. That, however, is not the way of life you learned when you heard about Christ and were taught in him in accordance with the truth that is in Jesus. You were taught, with regard to your former way of life, to put off your old self, which is being corrupted by its deceitful desires; to be made new in the attitude of your minds.[123]

If this all sounds familiar, it should. It is what is happening today as the world slips farther and farther away from God. We all must continually check to see if our hearts are hardened by the changing world and worldly values that we are subjected to each day.

---

[123] (NIV).

CHAPTER 8

# THE NATURAL AND THE SUPERNATURAL GIFTS OF GOD

## The Gifts of the Holy Spirit

FIRST CORINTHIANS 12:4 TELLS US that there are many different gifts, but they all come from the same Holy Spirit. While the gifts belong to Him, the Holy Spirit abides in me as a believer, which means I have His gifts abiding in me.

Many Protestant denominations today demonstrate a clear wariness of this topic. Without pointing fingers, I can say that many churches don't address this vital aspect of the Trinity due to a concern of appearing Pentecostal and focusing too much on this one facet of the Trinity. In so doing, they then ignore or at least limit God's ability to work in the lives of believers and accomplish fully what He can do through the Holy Spirit.

In my personal walk with God on this journey, I quickly came to the realization that the closer the relationship I have with the Holy Spirit, the closer the experience I will have with the gifts of the Spirit, including the gift of healing the sick.

## The Holy Spirit Guides and Empowers Us

After a person is born again, or has accepted Christ as his or her Savior, the person must realize that this is only the beginning of a supernatural, spiritual life. God has given us more than we can even imagine.

## The Natural Gifts of God

Most Bible scholars will generally point to the twelfth chapter of Romans to identify the natural gifts of God:

> For just as each of us has one body with many members, and these members do not all have the same function, so in Christ we, though many, form one body, and each member belongs to all the others. We have different gifts, according to the grace given to each of us. If your gift is *prophesying*, then prophesy in accordance with your faith; if it is *serving*, then serve; if it is *teaching*, then teach; if it is to *encourage*, then give encouragement; if it is *giving*, then give generously; if it is *to lead*, do it diligently; if it is *to show mercy*, do it cheerfully.[124]

## The Supernatural Gifts of God

According to 1 Corinthians, the spiritual or supernatural gifts of God are as follows:

> Now about the gifts of the Spirit, brothers and sisters, I do not want you to be uninformed. You know that when you were pagans, somehow or other you were influenced and led astray to mute idols. Therefore I want you to know that no one who is speaking by the Spirit of God says, "Jesus be cursed," and no one can say, "Jesus is Lord," except by the Holy Spirit.

---

[124] Romans 12:4–8 (NIV), emphasis added.

There are different kinds of gifts, but the same Spirit distributes them. There are different kinds of service, but the same Lord. There are different kinds of working, but in all of them and in everyone it is the same God at work.

Now to each one the manifestation of the Spirit is given for the common good. To one there is given through the Spirit *a message of wisdom*, to another *a message of knowledge* by means of the same Spirit, to another *faith* by the same Spirit, to another *gifts of healing by that one Spirit*, to another *miraculous powers*, to another *prophecy*, to another *distinguishing between spirits*, to another *speaking in different kinds of tongues*, and to still another *the interpretation of tongues*. All these are the work of one and the same Spirit, and he distributes them to each one, just as he determines.[125]

## Supernatural Healings

Healings that are recorded in the Bible are often associated with the ministries of specific individuals, including Jesus, Elijah, Paul, and others. Clearly, no person has the power to heal anyone; instead, individuals utilize a supernatural gift through the Holy Spirit to accomplish the miraculous. Healings recorded in the gospels, such as the following verse from John, are often referred to as "signs" to demonstrate Jesus's divinity and to increase belief in Him as the Christ: "Unless you people see signs and wonders," Jesus told him, "you will never believe."[126]

---

[125] 1 Cor. 12:1–11 (NIV), emphasis added.
[126] John 4:48 (NIV).

## Jesus Told His followers to Heal the Sick

In Matthew 10:8 we read, "Heal the sick, raise the dead, cleanse those who have leprosy, drive out demons. Freely you have received; freely give."[127] One of the names of God found in the Old Testament is *Jehovah-Rapha,* which is translated as "I am the Lord who heals you." The word *Rapha* literally means to *restore* or to *make healthy* in the Hebrew language.

Many Bible scholars feel that Matthew 8:17 (NIV) was to fulfill what was spoken through the prophet Isaiah: Matthew 8:17 tells us that Jesus "took up our infirmities and bore our diseases."[128] Many Bible scholars feel that this verse fulfills what was spoken by the prophet Isaiah: "But he was pierced for our transgressions, he was crushed for our iniquities; the punishment that brought us peace was on him, and *by his wounds we are healed.*"[129] This prophecy is proof that Christ paid for *all* our healings on the cross, not just for our sins.

The New Testament documents that during Jesus's walk on earth and even after His Resurrection, His apostles healed the sick, cast out demons, made lame men walk, and many other miraculous things in His name and through His authority. At no time does the scripture say that these miracles ceased at the end of that age.

Today there are significant differences in belief about miraculous healing, even among people within the same denomination. As a result, there are many people in the church and, in fact, entire denominations that either partially or totally ignore this God-given gift.

When we reject or ignore this or any of God's gifts, we are putting God in a box. We are limiting God to only using one form of healing. God, however, is not limited by our minds or by our limited imaginations, and He is free to do whatever He desires. We

---

[127] (NIV).

[128] (NIV).

[129] Isaiah 53:5 (NIV), emphasis added.

must retrain ourselves to believe that God can heal in ways that go far beyond our simple human ability to comprehend.

As discussed in chapter 5, when someone is healed by the knowledge and skill of a doctor, this does not mean God has not healed the person. God knows what we need and whether we are best served by a miraculous healing or by one that conforms to the laws of nature. That decision is best left up to Him. And yes, the scriptures specifically note that the church is authorized to pray for healing in the name of Jesus: "Is any sick among you? Let him call for the elders of the church; and let them pray over him, anointing him with oil in the name of the Lord."[130]

---

[130] James 5:14 (KJV).

CHAPTER 9

# KEYS TO FINDING YOUR OWN MIRACLE

## Seeking God's Will above Our Own

FIRST AND FOREMOST ON MY journey to *My Own Miracle*, I learned that I needed to do it His way. I slowly learned to seek His will for my life. More than anything, I had to learn to trust in Him. God loves you. Jeremiah 29:11 says it so well: "'For I know the plans I have for you,' declares the Lord, 'plans to prosper you and not to harm you, plans to give you hope and a future.'"[131] Trust God for the healing or miracle that <u>He</u> wants for you, not for what you would have for yourself.

## Let Go and Let God: The Power of Total Surrender

One of the biggest challenges any of us face in our Christian walk is totally surrendering ourselves, and every part of our lives, to the Lord. Can you truly say that there are *no* areas in your life that you have not completely surrendered to Him and for Him rather than for yourself?

We have to be aware of surrendering that is selfishly motivated. That's not total surrender, that's a hoped-for exchange. If your

<hr>

[131] (NIV).

surrender is based on a well-intentioned offer to give something up in order to get something in return, then that is not total surrender; that's saying to God, "Let's make a deal."

For example, if you say, "I'm going to truly forgive someone God wants me to forgive because I want to receive healing *and* because I know my lack of forgiveness is standing in the way," your whole premise is wrong. Forgiving someone is the result of being right with God. Our motive for surrender should not be personal gain. That is *not* total surrender. We can become so self-centered that we turn to God because we want something from Him rather than because we want God Himself.

Total surrender will always go beyond our natural desires. More than ever before, we must beware of stopping short of total surrender to God. Most of us have the concept of what this means, but few of us have truly experienced it.

## Trust That God's Promises Are Timeless

What is active faith? Active faith requires action, not just words. Hebrews 13:7–8 says, "Remember your leaders, who spoke the word of God to you. Consider the outcome of their way of life and imitate their faith. Jesus Christ is the same yesterday and today and forever."[132] Imitating their faith would require putting feet to your faith, as some say, as "Faith without works is dead also."[133] You can say anything you want, but if you don't act on what you say, there will be no results.

Old timers used to say, "Saying is one thing, but doing is quite another." Similarly, Peter knew he had to do more than just believe and call out to Jesus during the storm; he had to step out of the boat to demonstrate his faith with his actions.

I'm a pilot, and to gain experience in my early days of flying I would volunteer to fly planeloads of skydivers, many of whom were

---

[132] (NIV).

[133] James 2:26 (KJV).

73

first-timers in training. While some would admit their fears, there would inevitably be that one tough guy who would boast about his total lack of fear and willingness to make his first jump. In those days, even first timers were allowed to make their first jump solo. They were under the direction of a certified instructor, and their ripcord was attached to a tether that would automatically open their parachute if they were to panic. I would fly the aircraft up several thousand feet, and the skydivers were required to climb out of the plane once we were at jumping altitude. Once they were outside of the plane, they would position themselves on a tiny step while holding on to the wing strut for support. Once the instructor was satisfied that the student was ready to release and begin his or her dive, the instructor would scream over the noise of the engine, "Jump!". You'd be surprised at how many of those tough guys (and women) would continue to hang on as the instructor screamed over and over, "Jump! Jump! Jump!" We had a foolproof way of sending them on their way: the instructor would turn to me and say, "Blow 'em off," at which point I would move the throttle from a setting just barely enough to keep the plane airborne to a full throttle setting. The massive blast of air coming from the propeller at that speed was so great that no one, no matter how strong, could withstand it. We often joked that we'd hear the first half of a bad word as the jumper's fear was overcome by my blasting him or her off of the side of the aircraft.

While that story may seem humorous, how many of us can say that we have totally trusted God in every instance and taken our own leap of faith without God having to do something to make us move?

We had a standard rule that those in training were to be called "students" rather than "skydivers" until they had completed their first jump. We the believers, like them, have not shown faith until we too take that leap of faith.

## Claim Your Healing!

If there is one area where we stumble when it comes to receiving healings, it is in the area of doubt. I have to wonder how many millions of miracles have gone unclaimed by believers who gave up just short of crossing the line and receiving what God had prepared for them. It is important that you make God's word *the* final authority in your walk with Him. You must become convinced in your heart that it is God's desire to bless you and that your healing is a purchased possession for you to claim.

One critical lesson that God reveals over and over again to me is to take more time listening and less time talking *to* Him. Perhaps you've heard the old adage that there is a reason why God gave us only one mouth but two ears. We should listen twice as much as we speak. Take time every day to be still, get quiet, and listen to the Lord. He desires to minister to you and encourage you, but He cannot do that while we are speaking. To receive is the opposite of to send; you cannot do both at the same time. Each of us needs to learn to recognize His voice.

As a hobby, I also am a ham radio operator, and I often think of an example someone once shared with me. He said that as a radio operator holds down the "transmit" button on the microphone, the operator cannot hear the person on the other end until he or she releases the button and listens. Radio operators routinely end what they are saying with the word "over" as they release the transmit button. It's a clear indication that they are about to stop speaking and begin listening. We also need to break up our prayers with "over" pauses as we stop talking and surrender the prayer airwaves to God. If you feel that God never speaks to you, you may need to ask yourself if you are really listening.

## Then Proclaim your Healing

One of the things I did on my journey was to *publicly* receive my healing by faith. I began by telling my wife, "I am healed," and then shared with others that God was in the process of healing me. Just as I wrote this book before the miracle was manifest in my body, I also claimed my healing by faith even before there was any evidence of it showing. I believe that doing so shows God our faith and helps abolish fear and disbelief.

When the devil attempts to convince you that you are not going to get healed, you need to do what Christ did and quote him the word of God. Then you can tell him, "Sorry, Devil, you're too late! I've already received my miracle by faith."

Remember that the devil is after your faith and wants you to believe in his ability to defeat the word of God in you. Don't fall for that old lie! Remind the devil that your body is the temple of the Holy Spirit and that through Jesus you are an overcomer.[134]

Boldly use God's word as the ruling authority in your life to come against the challenge you are facing. Chase off any doubt and oppression that may be harassing you. Just as you would defend your home from an invader, accept His authority over His temple (your body). Command the sickness to leave, and command your body to line up with the word of God. Tell Satan, "I am a believer and not a doubter." Luke 10:19 reminds us, "I have given you authority to trample on snakes and scorpions and to overcome all the power of the enemy; nothing will harm you."[135]

## Don't Compromise Your Stance

James 1:6–7 says it all: "But when you ask, you must believe and not doubt, because the one who doubts is like a wave of the sea, blown and tossed by the wind. That person should not expect to receive anything from the Lord."[136]

---

[134] 1 Cor. 10:19.
[135] (NIV).
[136] (NIV).

## Believe by Faith

As 2 Corinthians 5:7 says, "We live by faith, not by sight."[137] I once heard someone say that walking by faith means living your life in light of eternal consequences. Walking by faith means that you follow God's promises and His word and that you honor God no matter what people say and no matter what other forms of evidence seem to indicate. This also means that we must obey the Bible even when it conflicts with human opinion, and we must choose righteousness over sin, no matter what the cost.

Living by faith is trusting in God in every circumstance and having faith that God rewards those who seek Him, regardless of what others may say. Hebrew 11:6 says, "But without faith it is impossible to please him: for he that cometh to God must believe that he is, and that he is a rewarder of them that diligently seek him."[138]

## Make God's Word the Final Authority in Your Life

You must become convinced in your heart of what the scriptures clearly state: healing is a purchased possession for you. Make up your mind that you will not settle for anything less than what God has promised for your life through His word.[139]

When the devil attempts to convince you that you are not going to get healed, just put a smile on your face and tell him he's too late, because you've already received it by faith!

Speak in line with the word of God regarding your situation. Don't focus on and speak about the problem; focus on and speak about the *answer*. We do not deny that sickness is present, but faith denies it the right to stay! Sickness has no right to stay in your body. First Peter 2:24 tells us, "He himself bore our sins in his body on the

---

[137] (NIV).
[138] (KJV).
[139] 1 Cor. 2:12; Rom. 4:20–22; Gal. 3:13.

cross, so that we might die to sins and live for righteousness, and; by his wounds you have been healed."[140]

## Make God Feel Welcome in Your Life through Praise

Make praise and worship daily parts of your life by rejoicing at your life in Christ and His promises. Christ deserves our adoration. Christ is everything we need, and it is He who gives us victory! Through praise and worship, it is much more natural to expect miracles and to be victory-minded. God lives through our praise: "Yet you are enthroned as the Holy One; you are the one Israel [your people] praises."[141]

## Change the Way You Think about Praying to God

Have you ever considered that God is not an answering machine or a request line? He's God, so He already knows your needs even before you can ask. Why then do we start prayers with a few words of thanks before unrolling our wish list prayer scroll? If you really want to change your prayer life, try this sometime: start your prayer with "Lord, what's on your heart for me today?" Then forget your list of desires and focus quietly on listening to His desires. This might be the first time this concept has ever crossed your mind! That's okay. Deuteronomy 4:29 promises that "if from there you seek the Lord your God, you will find him if you seek him with all your heart and with all your Soul."[142]

## Get a Daily Checkup

It is always a good idea to check yourself out before the Lord for any lack of forgiveness or any other doors you may have opened to the enemy. Once these issues have been identified, you then need

---

[140] (NIV).

[141] Psalm 22:3 (NIV).

[142] (NIV).

to repent and make changes as quickly as possible. Don't forget about the promise in 1 John 1:9 "that if we confess our sins, He is faithful and just to forgive us our sins and to cleanse us from all unrighteousness."[143]

Remember, sin will block the blessings of God, so get rid of all your blessing blockers!

## Read the Word Daily

Read the Word daily, and hide it in your heart. Each of us needs to practice daily devotions, Bible reading, learning, growing, and maturing, even when it feels difficult.

## Stand

At every opportunity, we need to stand steadfast in His promises and keep on standing! Dig your feet in and refuse to be moved from the truth of God's word.[144] As you stand, don't waver. As it says in James 1:6–7, "the person who wavers will not receive from God." And once you have done all that you can, put on God's full armor and "stand."[145]

## Keep Your Priorities Straight

Be careful not to let your healing become more important than your relationship to your heavenly Father. Don't allow it to become an idol. Keep the Lord, your relationship with Him, and your love for Him in first place in your life.

## Recognize That Our Power Is through Him

When Jesus slept in the midst of the storm that His disciples thought was the end of their lives, He did so knowing that His

---

[143] (NIV).
[144] Eph. 6:10–18.
[145] Eph. 6:13.

Father knew better. He knew His Father saw the storm they were in, and that He knew Jesus was with them. In fact, God saw beyond the storm and could see them safely on the other shore at the end of their journey. Jesus saw the storm as just one more opportunity to build faith and show His power when He commanded it to stop. Remember what the disciples' reaction was? They were astonished at what He was able to do and asked, "Who is this? Even the wind and waves obey him!"[146] What kind of men or women of God would people say we were if they saw our faith in action?

People are impressed by our testimony and God is honored when people see us take a risk and step out in faith.

## But I Am a Sinner!

A pastor friend of mine taught me a memorable lesson long ago about a verse in an old hymn that can be used in the wrong way. The lyrics say that you are only "a sinner, saved by grace." While the writer's intent was pure, the devil would like us to believe that we are still just sinners. The lyrics should change after our salvation to simply say that we are "saved by grace" and are therefore *new* creations in Christ![147] When we are saved, the old is gone.

Jesus doesn't mean that we cannot or do not ever sin again; rather, He means that we are new creations that no longer live in that sin. We ask forgiveness and move on. That is why we are reminded that it is important to put new wine in new wineskins.[148] Old wineskins are dry and unable to stretch; they will not expand with the new life of the contents they are filled with, so never attempt to live as a "sinner, saved by grace," but rather as a new creation, thankful for God's work of grace in your life.

Another way to think of this is to ask, "What can I fill up with God?" Only God can hold God's truth and preserve it. God's new

---

[146] Mark 4:41 (NIV).
[147] 2 Cor. 5:17.
[148] Matt. 9:17.

and divine nature is symbolic of the new wineskin, and it is His divine nature that we should seek when we are reborn. So if the devil attempts to remind you of your past, just remind the devil of his future! A good way to look at your daily walk is not to focus on being *like* Jesus but rather to remind yourself that because of what He did for you, you *are* like Jesus—a new creation who has access to the throne of the King of Kings!

You are *not* a remodeled version of your old self. I have personally remodeled many homes in my time, and if you strip off the new finishes of a remodeled home you'll always find the "bones" of the old house beneath a new look. When we are renewed in Christ, He promises that the old is demolished and we become new creations entirely.[149] Legalism says you still can sin, but Christ says the old sinful nature is gone. He says that when you do make a mistake, He will understand, help you turn from it, and help you desire not to make that mistake again.

God gives in abundant measure. James 1:5 says, "If any of you lack wisdom, you should ask God, who gives generously to all."[150]

## God's Love vs Our Love

Just before Jesus ascended, He taught us a powerful message about the love that He desires for us to follow. In John 21:15–17 Jesus asks Peter if Peter loves Him.[151] Peter clearly shows that he does not understand the type of love that God desires. He asks Peter, "Do you love me more than these?" and of course Peter replies, "Lord, you know that I love you." Jesus responds to him, "Feed my lambs." To his dismay, Jesus asks the question a second time, and again Peter responds, "Yes, Lord." When Jesus asks the question the third time, Peter is clearly hurt and responds, "Lord, you know all things; you know that I love you!"

---

[149] 2 Cor. 5:17.
[150] (NIV).
[151] (NIV).

As is often the case when we read any English translation of the scriptures, we don't fully understand the context of the question being asked or the statement being made. It is only when we research the Greek text that we fully understand the meaning of this section and Jesus's response. If we properly translate the word that Jesus used for *love*, we can see that Jesus asks Peter, "Do you agape me?" In modern Greek, *agape* is the love of God or God's love. This kind of love is God's covenant love for humankind and the way God desires us to love Him. It is unconditional love.

You will note then that when Peter responds, he says, "You know I *Phileo* you." *Phileo* is brotherly love. Jesus is asking Peter if Peter loves Him at God's level or humankind's level. God's love is far above human love, and we receive His love (agape) the moment we receive Him as our Lord and Savior. It is this love that separates us and sets us apart from the world. If you ever want to really study your relationship to God, ask yourself, "Do I love God unconditionally?" Then allow God to show you the "conditions" you may place on your love for Him.

## Peace

Jesus says, "Peace I leave with you, *my* peace I give you."[152] In times of trial, peace can seem elusive, but it's at times like these when we have to remind ourselves that one of the last things Jesus promised us when He walked the earth was that He left us with His peace. With that in mind, it's important to remember how wrong it would be to say, "I'm going to pray for His peace." He already has left His peace with us. We don't have to "try" to have His peace, because we already have it.

## Faith Is Not Faith without Action

Since the time of the cross, Christians have thought that we need to work to obtain more faith in order to reach the point where

---

[152] John 14:27 (KJV), emphasis added.

God will honor our request. God does not make any of His children work for miracles any more than He expects us to work for our salvation. There is nothing that we can offer that will earn our salvation, and nothing we can do will earn a miracle. Both salvation and miracles are gifts from our Father that we simply need to accept and believe in.

If you wouldn't dream of doubting your salvation, why then would you doubt His ability and His desire to give you your own miracle? You cannot work for your miracle; you need to believe and accept it!

The problem is that we live in a physical world that teaches us the exact opposite of faith. We are taught from an early age not to believe what we cannot see. In Mark 11:23, Jesus tells His believers (including you and me) that we can tell a mountain to be "removed" and it will be cast "into the sea." However, we tend to believe that we will be able to make that happen once we get the faith. Note what happened here? Jesus says to *say* it, and we say, "I will ... once I get the faith!" In other words, we are working to get what we want, but our work is *not* working! So our earthly minds are convinced that we do not have the faith, and we then compound our misery by—you guessed it—working harder and getting *more* frustrated.

In John 14:12, we find the truth that it's not about us working, it is about our faith and trust in *His* ability to do what we desire: "I tell you the truth, anyone who *has faith* in me will do what I [Jesus] have been doing [working miracles]. He [you] will do *even* greater things than these, because I am going to my Father."[153]

Imagine that! Jesus says you will be able to do even greater miracles than He has done! Remember, when Jesus walked the earth He walked on water, healed the sick, cast out demons, and even raised the dead, so how can it be that you or I could do greater miracles than those? Most commentaries state that the "greater" things referenced here refer to miracles that will be "in similar

---

[153] (NIV), emphasis added.

83

nature, but greater numbers" and that Jesus's reference to going to be with the Father is His assurance to His disciples that He will be leaving them with the Holy Spirit and the Holy Spirit's power to work miracles through His followers, including followers like you and me.

In similar fashion, we see in Luke 8 that Jesus, in the middle of a storm, sleeps in the boat as His disciples fear for their lives. They wake Him from His peaceful sleep with fearful cries and questions of why He is not doing something about the storm that is about to kill them. Jesus commands the storm to stop, peace returns, and then Jesus says to His disciples (and I believe that includes you and me), "Where is your faith?"[154]

After a study of numerous Bible commentaries, I found a common theme among interpretations of this verse: Jesus is not saying, "Why don't you have faith?" Instead He asks, "Why is it that you *have* faith, but you *use* none of it?" This is similar to standing in the middle of a huge fire with a fire hose in your hand. Instead of turning it on, you stand there as your life is at risk, telling the firefighters you are about to die! I'm not a firefighter, but I would imagine their response would be, "But you have what you need to save yourself right there in your hand! Use it!"

What we need is to *use* the faith that was birthed in us when we accepted Christ. We've all heard James 2:17 quoted: "Faith by itself, if not accompanied by action, is *dead*."[155] As I type this verse, my healing has not yet occurred. If it has begun, it is not yet visible to me or to my team of doctors. God said, "Write the book," so *in faith* I type these words, trusting fully that my God will honor His word and the words of His Son. I trust fully that I will get my own miracle.

Imagine if I had begun writing this book and offering you this advice only once I had actually seen evidence of a miracle. Would

---

[154] Luke 8:25 (NIV).
[155] (NIV).

that be faith? God wants me to act on faith, and He wants the same from you. Look not at the diagnosis (past) or the current conditions (present); look with faith to the future, and put your faith into action! Be like the centurion who sought out Jesus and said, "My servant lies at home paralyzed, suffering terribly." When Jesus asks, "Shall I come and heal him?" the centurion shows his great faith in action when he tells Jesus that He does not need to come to the centurion's home: "just say the word and my servant will be healed."[156] We see Jesus react to this show of great faith in verse 10: "Truly I tell you, I have not found anyone in Israel with such great faith." We then see Jesus's further reaction to this great faith when He tells the centurion in verse 13, "Go! Let it be done just as you believed it would." The servant is healed completely at that very moment!

Before the devil attempts to corrupt your understanding of this concept and tells you that you'll never have enough faith, remember that you're not the first person to struggle with your level of faith.

Remember the father in Mark 9 who brings Jesus his son who is "possessed by a spirit?"[157] Jesus's disciples cannot drive out the spirit, so He asks them to bring the child directly to Him. The son immediately begins convulsing upon being brought into Jesus's presence.[158] It was then that Jesus reminds everyone that "everything" is possible for those who believe. Then we hear the often-quoted line from Mark 9:24 as the father exclaims with tears in his eyes: "Lord, I believe, help thou mine unbelief." Recognizing the father's honesty, Jesus immediately goes into action, casting out the demon with *His* ability, not the child's father's faith. When His disciples later question Jesus as to why they failed to cast out the demon, Jesus tells them (verse 29) "This kind can come out only by prayer and fasting," or in other words, by going directly to God for His guidance and help.

---

156 Matt. 8:5–9 (NIV).
157 Mark 9:17.
158 Mark 9:18–20.

It would have been easy for the disciples, when faced with this demon, to try harder and harder (working on their own strength rather than with God's authority), only to fail. And they failed not because of their lack of faith, but because they had not taken it to the Lord in prayer, which they had earlier been taught to do. Prayer brings us into God's presence and gives us access to His guidance and authority.

When facing the impossible, remember Jesus's own words: "With man this is impossible; *but with God all things are possible.*"[159] Keep reminding yourself that you are not working with *your* authority. Because you are His child through Christ Jesus, you are acting with His authority in His mighty name with His power and His ability to do the impossible.

---

[159] Matt. 19:26 (NIV), emphasis added.

# CHAPTER 10

# WHEN GOD DOES NOT ANSWER

## Maintaining the Right Attitude During the Trials

I'D BE LESS THAN HONEST if I didn't confess that during my life I have struggled with doubt about whether God was really listening to me. It's understandable to ask, "Is God really there?" or "Is He really listening to me?" or "Will He ever respond?" or even the big one, "Is there really a God?"

As I went through my original diagnosis, I'll admit that the devil used every opportunity to tell me that I was a fool to believe in a God who was seemingly so distant and elusive. It was easy for doctors to quickly pass off issues as being related to Parkinson's once they found that word anywhere on my chart. Even friends and those close to me seemed to want to look for and find the worst for me. At least that is the way it felt at times.

Often I would recall the story of Job, a man who God dearly loved, and his battle that lasted a considerable portion of his adult life. I would look to his example of faith and endurance, and I would remind myself that God rewarded him twofold in the end. Even Job felt at times (often for good reason) that those close to him had let him down.

Elijah was another godly man who stayed faithful to God during hardship; in Elijah's scenario, God held back rain from the people for over three long years because of their sins.[160] You can only imagine how stressful it was for Elijah during that time. For three and a half years, as the people continued to live in sin, Elijah continued to hold on by faith while God was completely silent. God was not speaking even to His servant Elijah during this time of trial.

## Have You Ever Been to a Place Where the Silence of God Is Deafening?

Imagine what Elijah must have been going through as he waited. The silence and apparent separation from God must have seemed unbearable to him. Elijah was not liked, he was even an outcast, and yet the one who he trusted most was seemingly absent. Even though God would do a miracle through Elijah, Elijah could do nothing but have faith and wait.

Having sat through countless hours of counseling with people, I can honestly say that I have never found an honest believer who has not gone through such times. It can seem hopeless when God seems nowhere to be found.

## Don't Demand to Understand

It's much easier to celebrate a miracle than to endure the apparent lack of one. The hardest times in life are figuring out what to do during the days, weeks, months, or even years of silence.

As I mentioned elsewhere in the book, it is important to be honest with God. He knows us better than we know ourselves, and you won't offend Him by being honest about your struggle with His apparent silence. Ignoring it won't make it go away. A good thing to do to counter this type of negative thinking is to take note of all the times when God has come through in your past after a period of apparent silence.

Remember what God's word says in Isaiah 55:8–9: "For my

---

[160] 1 Kings 18:1.

thoughts are not your thoughts, neither are your ways my ways, declares the Lord. As the heavens are higher than the earth, so are my ways higher than your ways and my thoughts than your thoughts."[161] Just because you don't understand what He is doing does not mean that He is not working on your behalf, because He is. But trust Him, as He does it His way!

## "I Give Up" Is Different From "I Quit!"

During times of silence it is easy to be filled with fear, and if the trial goes on long enough, it can result in saying, "That's it! That's all I can take. I give up." Giving up can sometimes be the best thing that can happen to you when you finally reach a point where you "Let go and let God." A word of caution, however: when we let go, we must not harden our hearts and *quit*. Remember that when God is not answering, He is also not saying no to our request. Remind yourself that what seems to be "no" is more likely to be "not now."

## Wait with Anticipation

God is faithful, and one day He'll reveal His plans to you. Wouldn't it be a shame to quit and find out that the answer to your prayer was about to be revealed the very next day?

## While You Wait, Prepare to Receive

God will ultimately respond with His answer to your request, and because He is an all-knowing and perfect God, His plans will exceed your wildest dreams. You can always trust in His word, His judgment, and His desire to help you.

## Don't Waste Time Fighting Battles That Have Already Been Won!

I am no different from you or anyone who has gone through a

---

[161] (NIV).

time of trial. The devil tries to throw doubt, confusion, pain, and problems my way too, but I've made up my mind that I'm not going to assist him. In fact, the best thing we can do is to resist him. He may pick the fight, but the joke's on him: the battle is already over, and we have victory in Jesus.

On my journey, I have learned that it's always best to refuse him and not to dwell on what he has to say about my situations. He is the father of liars, so the last thing we should do is waste even a second by giving him our ear.[162]

I once overheard a dear family member warning another person, "Don't speak that into existence." She was absolutely right. When we speak something as truth, we can make it a reality. So if you think, "I might have [fill in the disease]," be careful not to give the devil the opportunity to make "I might have" into "I do have."

Earlier in my journey I even had doctors tell me (because someone else had written it on my chart) that my symptoms "seemed" to match those of a person with Parkinson's. I will also never forget the words of one doctor who scoffed after reading a chart sent to him by another of my physicians. He tossed the chart and results aside and said, "If all you have to work with is a hammer, everything starts looking like a nail." A word of caution here: I am *not* saying not to listen to your doctors, but then again, no reputable physician would be angered by your getting a second opinion, especially if the original testing was questionable, as mine was.

## Use God's Strength, Not Your Own!

God never instructs us to fight the devil with our own strength. He already empowered us and gave us victory over all the works of the enemy when He sent Jesus Christ to the cross for us. Given this, why should any of us fight with an enemy who has already been defeated? Or worse yet, why should we give him ammunition to fight us with?

---

[162] John 8:44.

James gives us clear instruction: "Submit yourselves therefore to God. Resist the devil, and he [the devil] will flee from you. Draw nigh [near] to God, and he will draw nigh to you."[163]

When Jesus died on the cross as the sacrifice for our sins, He also redeemed us from Satan's power: "And having disarmed the powers and authorities, he made a public spectacle of them, triumphing over them by the cross."[164]

When Satan tries to plant seeds of doubt when you are at your weakest point, rebuke him and remind him that he is already a defeated enemy! His legal authority was destroyed forever by the work of Christ on the cross.

Remember, *never* fight with an enemy who is already defeated!

---

[163] James 4:7–8 (KJV).
[164] Col. 2:15 (NIV).

# CHAPTER 11

# HINDRANCES TO MIRACLES

## Tolerated Sin or Sin That Has Not Been Confessed

WHILE SIN HAS BEEN AROUND since the Garden of Eden, sin that has not been confessed is perhaps the most common communication barrier between God and us. Psalm 66:18 says, "If I regard iniquity in my heart, the Lord will not hear me."[165] If we knowingly tolerate sin in our lives, it hinders our relationship with a perfect God who cannot tolerate sin. Today sin abounds and is becoming more and more acceptable to society as people turn away from God's desires and more toward their own desires. God's standards never change, however, and we're admonished not to make any provision for sin. Romans 13:14 clearly tells us what God expects us to do: "Put ye on the Lord Jesus Christ, and make not provision for the flesh, to fulfill the lusts thereof."[166]

The Internet is a powerful tool in many ways, but just as with any tool that can be used for good, it can also be used for evil. As we move into these last days and the coming of our Lord, the Internet, social media, movies, television, print media, and other sources of information are becoming worldlier, less godly, and in many ways trash bins filled with sin, profanity, pornography, and anti-Christian

---

[165] (KJV).
[166] (KJV).

rhetoric. We cannot continue to allow the constant influence of sinful information to stream into our homes and expect God's relationship with us to grow. The good news is that when we turn away from and confess sin, God is faithful and forgives us. Jeremiah 31:34 says, "For I will forgive their wickedness and will remember their sins no more."[167] God is able to do what we cannot. He will not only forgive our sins, but also He can "remember them no more." When we confess our sin and turn from it, our relationship to God becomes restored and our prayers again regain their power.

## Disobedience

Another hindrance that affects our relationship to our heavenly Father is disobedience. To grow in our relationship with God and expect Him to respond to our prayers, we *must* learn to obey. Turning from sin is the beginning of obedience, but keeping free from sin is the next step. If we confess with our mouths that we believe, but our actions don't match our words, it shows we don't really mean what we say. One of my favorite sayings is, "Your walk talks, and your talk talks, but your walk talks louder than your talk talks."

Here is another of my favorite sayings: "What you are when you are all alone and no one sees you is what you are."

Obedience is a natural outgrowth of faith in God.

## Selfish Desires

In John 15:7 we can see what a healthy relationship with God looks like: "If you remain in me and my words remain in you, ask whatever you wish, and it will be done for you."[168] God's desire is that we be one with Him just as our arms are a part of our bodies. When we function as one, there is harmony. If, however, we choose to place our will above His, we alienate ourselves from Him and cannot expect that "whatever [we] wish ... will be done for [us]."

---

[167] (NIV).
[168] (NIV).

Tremendous power is associated with surrendering our will to God. We receive the power of Christ through the Holy Spirit as we work as a team, following God's will rather than our own.

## Selfish Motives

Selfish motives show through in our prayer lives. James 4:3 sums it up quite well: "When you ask, you do not receive, because you ask with wrong motives, that you may spend what you get on your pleasures."[169] It is critical in each of our prayer lives to constantly ask, "Is this *my* desire or God's desire for me?"

## Mixed-Up Priorities

Every day we are each faced with choices: what things we buy, watch, participate in, or do are all awaiting our selection. If we are not careful to monitor our choices, we can easily get our priorities askew. We can even create idols that take God's place. If God places such a concern on your heart, ask yourself, "Would I be willing to give this up if God asked me to?" If there is anything that you place above God or would not surrender if He asked you to, then it's a hindrance that is blocking your communication to (and relationship with) Him.

## Not Loving One Another

John 13:34 commands us, "Love one another. As I have loved you, so you must love one another."[170] You'll note that the statement is unqualified. It does not tell us to love our family, friends, people we like, and so on. It simply commands us to love one another. So powerful is this command that in verse 35 it even becomes a testimony to others: "By this everyone will know that you are my disciples, if you love one another."

---

[169] (NIV).
[170] (NIV).

It breaks my heart when pastors tell me that one of their biggest struggles is with church members who not only fail to demonstrate that they love their pastors but also are actually their pastors' biggest critics. If this is hard for you to believe, keep in mind that John 13:34–35 was written to believers. If you struggle to love a pastor, another believer, or anyone, for that matter, try this: don't pray for the person without first asking God how He would desire you to pray as it relates to both of you!

By surrendering to this command, we can actually fulfill God's desire for us while we learn to love others. Prayer builds compassion. If you don't believe this, try to criticize someone you are praying for. The Holy Spirit will quickly intervene and show you the contradiction in your heart.

## Disregard for God's Sovereignty

When Christ died on the cross, we no longer were separated from the throne of God. We in no way should consider this new access as anything less than having the ability to approach the King of Kings and Lord of Lords.

When Jesus shows the disciples how to pray, the first thing He does is teach them how to honor God for who He is: "Our Father who art in heaven, hallowed be thy [your] name, thy kingdom come, thy will be done on earth as it is in heaven."[171] This is a clear acknowledgement that God is God! He is in charge, He is sovereign and almighty, and this prayer establishes our relationship to Him and with Him. We are children under the authority of our Father.

## A Lack of Forgiveness

If we desire an unhindered relationship with God, we must have spirits of forgiveness in our hearts.

We, as believers, have been forgiven for the greatest of offenses: we have willfully sinned against God. Each of us who has accepted

[171] Matt. 6:9–10 (KJV).

Christ as our Savior has been forgiven for transgressing the law of God. Yet we are often quick to anger and slow to forgive our fellow man or woman for the smallest of transgressions. Even the greatest sins committed against us are nothing when compared to how we have sinned against God. In Mark 11:25 Jesus says it clearly: "And when you stand praying, if you hold anything against anyone, *forgive them*, so that your Father in heaven may forgive you your sins."[172]

Many books have been written on this subject, and it is clear that we must guard our hearts to ensure that we are not harboring anger or resentment toward others. If we lack forgiveness, we should expect our prayers to be hindered.

While I am aware that I already covered this topic elsewhere in this book, I cannot stress this point too highly. On my journey of writing this book, God showed me over and over again the people in my life whom I had not forgiven and whom I held things against; He did this when I asked Him to bring them to mind. I'd also be less than honest if I did not say that once they were revealed to me, it was easy to truly forgive them—and once I did, God lifted the damage done. I cannot tell you how freeing this became. I am truly convinced that the enemy has no bigger weapon against us than blocking our spirits from forgiveness.

---

[172] (NIV), emphasis added.

# CHAPTER 12

# LESSONS LEARNED
## ALONG THE JOURNEY

## Misunderstanding God's Will

HOW MANY TIMES HAVE YOU heard someone pray, "Lord, if it is in Your will, please let this healing [or other miracle] occur"? Likewise we have all heard someone talk about "seeking God's will" on a certain matter. The error in this way of thinking is that it assumes that God's will is somehow unknowable or a secret, when in fact it is not.

God's will is outlined in the Lord's Prayer: "Thy will be done on earth as it is in heaven." That which is active "in heaven" is what God desires as His will for us now on earth!

In heaven we can expect health instead of sickness, joy instead of sorrow, and peace instead of stress and turmoil.

Just as we know sin is not in heaven and must therefore be cast out of our lives, God's will is that we also utilize His power and His authority to bind and cast out our sickness, spiritual bondage, depression, fear, sickness, anxiety, and so on. A simple test of God's will is to ask if a certain behavior or condition would be allowed in heaven. If the answer is no, then it should not be allowed in our bodies or our spiritual lives. *That* is God's will.

With this understanding, we don't need to ever say, "God, is this sickness in your will?" The Lord's Prayer clearly says it's not! His will is "as it is in heaven," and there is no sickness in heaven! When we come to the realization that God joins us in His will—that sickness is not His will, but health for our bodies and our minds is—the whole picture changes, and we soon see a new image of who we are in Christ. We see that in Him it is natural to cast out sin and sickness.

As believers, we must come to the realization that God's "normal" and our "normal" are almost never the same. With this in mind, we have to redefine *our* sense of what is and is not normal. If we begin by basing "normal" on our experience, then we are automatically limiting God; His normal is in the supernatural realm, while ours is based only in our experiences. If we realize that we are indeed God's people and empowered to do His will on earth, we can experience His "normal," which is as far above and beyond ours as possible.

Our expectation of what is normal is generally based only on the natural, but if we open our eyes and our expectations to God's vision and expectations, we can experience His normal (the supernatural) in our daily walk and in our experience. Jesus demonstrated this during His walk on earth. He did not view the miracles He performed as impossible, but instead He saw them as natural, attainable, and normal to His experience.

Christians should have a strong desire to seek out and to receive the impossible, because "with God *all* things are possible."[173]

---

[173] Mark 10:27 (KJV).

CHAPTER 13

# AND THE ANSWER CAME

WHILE I WAS READING ROMANS 4 one cold and gloomy lunch hour in November of 2012, the Holy Spirit gently spoke to me. As I read about Abraham's relationship to God, I saw myself and the mistakes I had been making reflected in the text.

Abraham might be called our first father in the faith, and he demonstrates the correct relationship we should have with our heavenly father. Abraham joined God in what God was doing for him, which was the turning point for him. He trusted God to set him on the right path instead of trying to be right on his own. Just like Abraham, if we see that the job is too big for us and that it's something only God can do, we must trust God to do it.

I was not fully trusting God in my health dilemma; instead, I was attempting to use Him as only a part of my team. That is as futile a concept as the bumper stickers you see on some cars that say, "God is my copilot." What foolishness! As a pilot myself, I know that a copilot is not in primary control of an aircraft; he or she takes the second seat and is called upon only to assist when needed. The captain is in charge, sets the course, takes the controls, and pilots the aircraft. Why was I putting God in the copilot's seat in my life and in *this* situation? While I was not doing it intentionally, I was doing it! It is only in trusting God that we, like Abraham, are set in a right-relationship with God, by God.

The answer I had longed for was waiting in these timeless scriptures. Just as He did for Abraham, God has big plans for those who will trust Him. Just as Abraham needed to first take the title "father," I too needed to take the title "healed by my Father." I too had to dare to trust God to do that which He, and *only* He, could do! This also meant that I had to let go of all my preconceived ideas about the ways that God might choose to accomplish my healing. If Jesus could raise Lazarus from the dead and restore his physically dead body back to perfect health, then I needed to trust the same Jesus to work a miracle His way and bring me back to health.

I needed to be like Abraham. When he was faced with the hopeless situation in his life, he believed anyway! That is faith: believing anyway! Even when faced with the most impossible, the most hopeless of situations, the faithful continue to believe. Just like Abraham, if I wanted to have God's blessings, I needed to trust Him and live not on the basis of what I saw that I could *not* do but instead on what God said *He* would do!

If any one of us truly wants to be blessed by God, we must surrender *all* and give up our own ambitions for His desires. I needed to stop trying to find my own path to a cure and instead accept the one He was waiting to freely give me. To demonstrate faith, I needed to put my faith where my mouth was. I had to stop putting on false fronts and replace my lack of faith with total trust in Him, speaking boldly of what God *would* do for me instead of what He was not doing in my situation.

As Christians draw closer to the end of this age, it's more important than ever that we walk by faith and by His promises. We are commanded to "live by faith, not by sight" and not to have a dependence on feelings and circumstances.[174] We must focus our gaze on unseen things and all of God's promises. God wants us to have

---

[174] 2 Cor. 5:7 (NIV).

faith and to "fix our eyes not on what is seen, but on what is unseen, since what is seen is temporary, but what is unseen is eternal."[175] As believers, we must demonstrate faith that is beyond our own ability and keep our eyes on His promises until they become reality.

Our entire Christian lives are a fight to stay in faith (see 1 Timothy 6:12 and 2 Timothy 4:7). Proverbs 3:5–6 tells us, "Trust in the Lord with all your heart and lean not on your own understanding; in all your ways submit to him."[176] Simply put, when we walk by faith, we are living and acting as though God's word is true *right now*. Hebrews 11:6 sums it all up: "Without faith it is impossible to please God, because anyone who comes to him must believe that he exists and that he rewards those who earnestly seek him."[177]

The first answer to my search for my own miracle was found in Romans 4: I had to trust God and "call that which did *not* exist [my healing] as though it *did* exist."[178] I had to stop looking at what was in front of me and stop believing that my situation was hopeless and would not change. I needed to start walking in faith! I needed to surrender *all* of myself to Him and to allow Him, and Him alone, to change the situation.

Second, I had to publicly share my struggle and talk as though He was already in the process of healing me and answering my prayer! I had to admit that instead of doing what God's word promises and "calling those things that do not exist as though they did," I was calling those things that *are* (or were) as if they would always be! It requires *no* faith at all to live that way! To do so is to live as the world does, and what a poor example we lead when we live by fear and perceived reality rather than by faith in the God we profess! Doctors, for example, are wonderful, but they are bound to tell you what they see as your situation; rarely will they ever "risk" bringing God into their discussions with you. Due to legalities and their fear

---

[175] 2 Cor. 4:18 (NIV).
[176] (NIV).
[177] (NIV).
[178] Emphasis added.

of lawsuits, they have learned to only discuss scientifically valid and documented facts with patients. While this is understandable in the litigious society we live in, it does not recognize the very real truth that we are made up of body and spirit.

Jesus tells us that we can have what we trust in God to give us. In Mark 11:24 we read, "Therefore I tell you, whatever you ask for in prayer, *believe that you have [already] received it, and it will be yours.*"[179] You will note that He does not say it "might be yours," "could be yours," "will be yours if you ask in just the right way," and so on; He simply says that it "*will* be yours" if you "believe that you have received it!" I had to believe I had already received it. I had to begin acting, talking, and expecting as though God had answered my prayers, even if it seemed as though nothing had changed! To receive from God, we must continually ask (with expectation) for what we don't see. When we do this, we are initiating God's faith in our lives.

If we look at the life of Abraham, we see that God changed Abram's name to Abraham. Abraham went from being called "exalted father" to "father of a multitude," even though he had no children of his own. Abraham and his wife Sarah named—or called—those things that did not exist as though they did for over twenty-five years before seeing God's promise fulfilled in their lives.

If you're faced with the impossible, begin talking and believing as though God has already answered your prayer. Act as though God has received your prayer and has responded or is in the process of responding in your favor. Faith works the same way in every area of life. Don't give up, and don't stop "calling those things that do not exist as though they did" until you see the manifestation of God's promises.

As Galatians 6:9 reminds us, "And let us not be weary in well doing: for in due season we shall reap, if we faint not."[180]

---

[179] (NIV), emphasis added.
[180] (KJV).

# CHAPTER 14

# My Own Miracle

I T WAS IN THE SUMMER of 2015 that I received the first tiny glimpse of change happening. The change was not in my body but in the way that I was thinking. This is where the story of *My Own Miracle* began to be revealed to me.

## Miracle 1: God Dreams

Unlike what you might think of as a miracle healing, I was about to receive miraculous wisdom and information that would ultimately lead to a life without tremors. Some might say that I didn't receive a miracle but rather a "process of healing." I would remind them that the condition I had (which the doctors would ultimately diagnose as benign essential tremor) is incurable. Therefore, I *did* receive healing brought about by information miraculously shared from heaven, without which I would not be tremor-free today!

While I can't remember the exact date, sometime in 2014 I began having a series of what I like to refer to as "God dreams." This was the first sign that I was receiving a response to my prayers for my own miracle.

In the first dream I was given a tiny glimpse of heaven. Lasting only a few seconds God allowed me to experience what heaven will be like. In those few precious moments I felt what God's love feels like in its truest form. It was by far the most real and vivid dream

I have ever had. It was as though love filled every cell of my body to the point that there was no room for anything else. Where there had been fear, there was now only peace; where there had been pain, there was now perfect health; and where there had been doubt, there was now the total absence of doubt as I experienced true faith or what might better be called "faith realized." I told you earlier that this first dream of heaven lasted only a few seconds, and looking back I now know why. If I had been allowed any more time, I most likely would not have come back! There are some things in our Christian walks that cannot be explained, and I am afraid that this is one of them, so I won't attempt to, but I can say this: heaven is wonderful, and one day we'll all understand!

This initial dream was later followed by numerous dreams that I could best describe as "knowledge downloads." While my doctorate is in psychology, my education in medical science is limited. Each one of these "knowledge downloads" was as if God were transferring medical knowledge directly into my mind, not so that I'd be able to use the information as a medical doctor would but, rather, so that I could understand what had been happening in my body that ultimately resulted in and caused the tremors. With this additional information, much of which was far beyond my ability to comprehend, I began a new relationship with God as He guided me to and through this process His way.

No, I will not tell you that I audibly heard God's voice speak to me, but with each new dream came the realization that God would not heal me in the way I thought He would. Rather, *He would use me to tell others that we should allow God to work in ways that we do not understand to accomplish His will in each one of us.*

Today there are far too many men and women ready to tell you what God "told" them. In the New Testament alone I have found dozens of times in which we are warned not to speak on God's behalf, specifically as it relates to prophecy (that is, of course, unless the people doing so truly have the gift of prophecy). Turn on almost any Christian network channel these days and listen closely to how often the person speaking says that God told, revealed, spoke, let him or her see the future, and so on. While some may well be telling the truth, scripture clearly warns that we are to be very careful: "Beloved, believe not every spirit, but try the spirits whether they are of God: because many false prophets are gone out into the world."[181] In Matthew 7:15 we are told to "beware of false prophets, who come to you in sheep's clothing but inwardly are ravening wolves."[182] And in 2 Peter 2:1 we are warned that there will be false prophets and false teachers who will bring about "swift destruction."

Why then do I tell you this? Simply stated, I want you to see how hesitant I am to share with you what He has shared with me. As I write this, my prayer is that I never speak for Him but rather only state these things He has shown me. As you have been taking your own journey, I have attempted to show you things that He has allowed me to see and experience so that you can also look to Him, on your own, for your opportunities to learn from Him as well.

Aided by the new information God shared with me during my knowledge downloads, I began hundreds of hours of research. Taking what had been given to me in the dreams, I combed through countless medical journals, researching clues contained within the dreams.

Turning at times to doctors for additional research and support for my theories, I met with a full spectrum of responses ranging from support to skepticism to even outright anger at times. More than a few times I was politely told that I was wasting my time. After all, if the greatest minds in medical science couldn't find a cure for this "incurable" disease, what made me think that I stood any chance of finding one? The truth is that I had on my team *the* greatest mind in the entire universe, the Great Physician! Once I was able to get past my self-imposed barriers, I could allow God the freedom to work both in and through me, and that He did.

---

[181] 1 John 4:1 (KJV).
[182] (KJV).

Unlike perhaps every other book on healing ever written, *My Own Miracle* is the story of how God can and does operate on an *individual* basis in each of our lives. Instead of working in a predetermined way, God grants miracles differently in each of our lives. In short, God likes to create your *own* miracle, just for you!

## Overcoming My Own Understanding of Miracles

Like many people, I had a picture in my mind of the way God performs miracles. You go to a meeting with other believers, someone who has the gift of healing prays for you, and then you receive your miracle! As I mentioned earlier in the book, while many times this is the case, what about all of those who attend the meetings and do not receive healing? Are they left out? Doesn't God love them? Isn't He going to grant their desire? Is He turning down their request?

I say all of these things for a reason. Because I have attended such meetings and felt all of the above, God moved me to write this book and explain that while He can work at such healing sessions, *He is not limited to working only in this manner.* Furthermore, more often than not He responds to each person's needs on an individual basis. God is not limited by the constraints we place upon Him. Just as He can heal at a church meeting, He can also heal someone in a hospital bed, an emergency room, a car driving down the road, the middle of a crowded restaurant, or a room all alone.

God is above and beyond all that we can think or imagine, so we should not limit Him or put Him in a box. Yet each of us does that when we restrict Him by our personal beliefs, myself included.

My own miracle did not occur at a church gathering, with anyone else present, or in a way that I had ever perceived possible. In Chapter 5 I explained all the ways that God heals us. Again, some might be tempted to say that I did not receive a miracle in the sense prescribed by their traditional way of thinking. My miracle came to me through the God dreams mentioned earlier.

Based on information I learned through the God dreams, I began studying a relatively new technique, which at the time had only been approved by the government, called deep brain stimulation, or DBS for short. According to the Mayo Clinic, "Deep brain stimulation involves implanting electrodes within certain areas of your brain. These electrodes produce electrical impulses that regulate abnormal impulses. The electrical impulses can affect certain cells and chemicals within the brain. The amount of stimulation in deep brain stimulation is controlled by a pacemaker-like device placed under the skin in your upper chest. A wire that travels under your skin connects this device to the electrodes in your brain."[183] Deep brain stimulation is now used to treat a number of neurological conditions, including the condition that I have, benign essential tremor.

About now you are probably saying to yourself, "But wait a minute; I thought this book was about miracles, and here you are telling me about using modern medicine to resolve this issue." Again, reread chapter 5, and pay special attention to the second way in which God is able to work *through* doctors and *through* medicines.

Chapter 5 reads, in part,

> Now let's give thanks to those who practice medicine and assist God in healing. As the Bible says, "Every good and perfect gift is from above, coming down from the Father of the heavenly lights, who does not change like shifting shadows."[184]

> God heals through doctors and through medicines, surgeries, therapies, treatments, and so on. But the key here is that *they* don't do the healing; God does!

---

[183] "Deep Brain Stimulation," *Mayo Clinic*, November 11, 2015, http://www.mayoclinic.org/tests-procedures/deep-brain-stimulation/home/ovc-20156088.
[184] James 1:17 (NIV).

Using doctors does not show a lack of faith. Remember that God created doctors, and He can use them in caring for our earthly bodies. It is also commonly believed that Luke was a physician. Paul calls him "the beloved physician," and undoubtedly one reason for his ongoing association with Paul was Paul's need for frequent medical care.[185] Paul speaks of a medical problem that he calls a "thorn in the flesh," for example, and he also speaks about his "infirmities."[186]

In Jesus's day, He endorsed the medical practices of the time, such as the use of oil and wine. We see Jesus praise the Good Samaritan for acting like a physician, and He tells His disciples to go and do the same.

With all of this in mind, I felt led by the Spirit of God that, at least for the time being, this would be my answer, and if need be, this would also be my "thorn in the flesh," just as Paul describes his health challenge in 1 Corinthians 12:7.

Without denying God the chance to one day (totally) heal me, I was to take advantage of this opportunity and explore the technique of DBS.

## And So the Journey Began

It would be dishonest to not disclose how difficult this procedure would ultimately be, but at the same time I must disclose how faithful God was as I took this arduous journey. In fact, my wife and I saw God's hand working in ways that can only be described

---

[185] Col. 4:14.
[186] 2 Cor. 12:7, 9 (KJV).

as miraculous. Step-by-step, God was with us as we walked together down the long path and over seemingly unsurpassable obstacles.

## *The First Thing to Overcome Was Fear*

Did I really want to take a risk as great as this? After all, this involved not one but two surgeries, the first of which would be on my brain and which I had to be awake the entire time for! Yes, you heard it right. In order for the surgery to be a success, the patient needs to be fully awake for the entire surgery, which in my case lasted almost eight hours! You see, tremors disappear when a person goes to sleep or is sedated. Since the brain has no nerve endings and feels no pain, this surgery is generally done with the patient fully awake. The only medication that would be used to ease pain would be the numbing medication I would receive at the site where the incisions were to be made on my scalp and where a frame would be attached to help the surgeons in this procedure.

## *Paying for the Surgery*

While I had good insurance through my workplace, the issue of coverage of such an extensive and relatively new procedure quickly became an obstacle and resulted in *nothing less than a miracle*. The first obstacle that quickly became a roadblock was the insurance company's insistence that they would not pay for the procedure if the tremors could be "effectively controlled" by medication. You can imagine the amount of time, effort, and money that was spent trying the myriad of medications, one at a time. Eventually the list was exhausted, all without any real success. Then there came the issue of getting the insurance company to actually pay for the surgeries, which resulted in a bill larger than what some people spend on a home mortgage.

We saw God work a *documented miracle* shortly after returning home after the second surgery.

Imagine my shock to get home and open a letter from a medical doctor who worked for the insurance company stating, in part, that he had reviewed all the bills from the hospital and ruled that the procedures done were not medically necessary and therefore were not covered!

Yes, both surgeries were now complete, and only then were they saying that they would not be covered. A quick call to my insurance agent only served to increase my fears that I would be forced to pay this gigantic bill myself. Quickly we went to the Lord in prayer, as we were once again in need of a miracle.

My insurance agent, who is also a believer and a close personal friend, said there were only two options: the first was to get the insurance company to change its mind and somehow pay for the surgeries; the second was to file an appeal with the state, asking that they force the insurance company to pay the bill. Neither option stood much of a chance.

## Miracle 2: Money

Without any real action on my part, the insurance company sent me a notification only a few weeks later that they would pay *the entire bill.* Praise God! If you've ever worked with companies like this before you *know* that this was nothing short of a miracle. I checked with the hospital shortly thereafter, and they verified that they had received payment but that we would be responsible for the co-payment. Again, I felt that cold chill run up and down my spine as I read on. I'll never forget my wife's response as she asked me what our co-payment would be. I responded, "Seven," to which she responded, "Seven thousand dollars?" I answered, "No, seven dollars." We both praised God for the miracle as I held up a note that she had earlier taped to our refrigerator. Her note read, "God is faithful!"

It wasn't until a week later that I was reminded that the seven-dollar co-pay was not by accident but by God's own hand, as seven is God's number. Without going into detail, entire books have been written on how the Bible signifies that the number seven is God's divine number showing His perfection and completeness. It was as if He had signed the bill Himself after paying it, reminding us of whose hand had made it all happen.

Then there was the issue of taking off work for two months for the surgery and recovery period. Keep in mind that at the time I was the president and CEO of one of the largest companies in America that provides homecare services to older adults. With an annual budget of almost $17 million and well over two hundred employees, you don't simply announce that you are going to take two months off without a *lot* of explaining. God was faithful here too, as He supplied me with an outstanding staff and a board of directors who stood by me, supported me, and filled the void while I was out of the office.

## Miracle 3: The Tremors Are Gone!

No words could describe how I felt or the look on my wife's face as I sat in the doctor's office about one month after the initial surgery and two physicians, working together, turned on the device that was now implanted within me. I sat trembling in the chair as they each looked at me and activated the device. Seconds passed, and each of us waited for a reaction. Keep in mind that I'd had tremors since I was only a small child and could not remember a time when they were *not* a part of me. The only way that I can describe it is to say that after a few seconds, I felt as if a small electrical shock went through me, followed quickly by a switch being turned off. The switch was like turning off a light (or in my case, a tremor), and in its place there was now a perfect calm and peace. Decades of tremors were now gone, and in their place was a sense of peace and calm that I cannot even begin to explain. It was as if God Himself laid His hand on the top of my head and said, "Peace."

Today I tell people that God is good and that He has allowed me to return to full functionality but that He has, as He did with Paul, left me with this one small "thorn in my flesh." If you were to look at me you'd say, "But Bob, what thorn? You are totally healed and I don't see any evidence of a tremor," to which I would say, "Watch what happens when I turn the unit off!" You guessed it: the tremor would return in a matter of seconds.

As we read about Paul's "thorn" in 2 Corinthians, we perceive that he receives it as a tool to keep him humble. We all could use that, right? So, for the time being, God had responded to my request, but as with Paul, He was telling me that He wanted to keep me close by His side. Paul's thorn shows how God can even take the things that seem like challenges and turn them into blessings and tools that He can use. It shows that God's grace was enough for Paul and that His power is made perfect in our weakness.

Today I am tremor free—praise God! If God chooses to heal me completely one day, or if He chooses to leave this one small "thorn in my flesh," I know that I serve a God who loves me and who has taught me volumes on the journey to *My Own Miracle.*

## CHAPTER 15

# ONCE HEALED

ONCE YOU HAVE RECEIVED A miracle, the journey has just begun. A miracle from God is not an ending; in fact, for someone who has received a healing, to end the journey at that point is not only wrong but selfish. God did not work a miracle in your life only to heal you but for you to be a witness and, yes, even to be a sign to others.

## What I Saw on the Journey

Along my journey I heard of a believer in ministry who was stricken with Parkinson's disease. His testimony was powerful, as he told of how he was instantly and miraculously healed totally of Parkinson's. My hope was buoyed by his testimony of a clear and obvious healing that could only have come from God, and I didn't hesitate a moment to try to contact him via his website. I was concerned when his website email system was unresponsive to my first request, and then my second and third email also went unanswered. Shortly thereafter his website disappeared entirely, and I located him through another source. Again, there was no answer to my repeated inquires.

While I was able to confirm that he is alive and his healing genuine, it broke my heart to see someone so richly blessed, but for whatever reason, reluctant to engage with other believers in need.

## "Blessed Are They That Have Not Seen, and Yet Have Believed."

As I was preparing to write this section, I was reminded of Thomas. Thomas is someone who walks with Jesus and sees His miraculous powers to heal, cast out demons, open blinded eyes, and even raise people from the dead. Yet when told that Jesus has risen from the dead, Thomas, a disciple of Jesus, literally demands to feel Jesus's wounds before he will be convinced.[187] It is only after seeing Jesus alive and being offered the chance to touch His wounds that Thomas professes his faith in Jesus's resurrection from the dead. Jesus responds to Thomas by saying, "Blessed are they that have not seen, and yet have believed." It shows the true nature of God that Thomas is not scolded by Jesus but is instead accepted and loved by Him as He gently tells him that God is touched by our pure faith.

As I thought about this and what role a person should play after being healed, I was convicted by something the Holy Spirit laid on my heart. Just like Jesus, once we have been healed it becomes our role to roll up our sleeves and expose our wounds. Those wounds on Jesus's wrists, feet, and side will be the only scars in heaven, and they will never go away because they are visible signs of God's miraculous power to heal us from sin, sickness, and all the injuries we sustain on this side of eternity. Our commitment to God both before and after receiving healing is to surrender our bodies as in Romans 12:1–2, which says, "Therefore, I urge you, brothers and sisters, in view of God's mercy, to offer your bodies as a living sacrifice, holy and pleasing to God—this is your true and proper worship. Do not conform to the pattern of this world, but be transformed by the renewing of your mind. Then you will be able to test and approve what God's will is—his good, pleasing and perfect will."[188]

Our role, especially after receiving healing from God, is not to scold others for their lack of belief. Our role is to be walking

---

[187] John 20:24–29.
[188] (NIV).

testimonies that show the world what Jesus did for us, just as He showed His own healing to Thomas. Jesus offered His body as living testimony when He said to Thomas, "Put your finger here; see my hands. Reach out your hand and put it into my side. Stop doubting and believe."[189] Jesus could have simply risen from the dead and returned to heaven, yet He offered Himself once again as living evidence so that others might believe, and when He did—well, look at the impact it had: "Thomas said to him, 'My Lord and my God!' and he believed!"[190]

Share your healing for nothing less than it is—living evidence that the same Jesus who appeared to Thomas is alive and still in the miracle-working business today!

---

[189] John 20:27 (NIV).
[190] John 20:28 (NIV).

# CHAPTER 16

# CLOSING

I'LL END THIS BOOK IN almost exactly the same way that I began it, by offering to you again the greatest miracle of all time. This is a miracle that won't just give you healing that lasts the rest of your life on earth; it will assure you of an eternity with God.

I believe that it is no accident that this book is in your hand. The same God who created you loves you more than you will ever know or be able to comprehend. It is He who is calling out to you at this very moment.

God loves you so much that He sent His only Son, Jesus Christ, to die in your place so that you could have the miracle of forgiveness of all your sins if you are willing to repent (which means to "turn from" your sins) and accept the sacrifice that He has already promised you in His Son, Jesus.

If you are feeling that God can't forgive you of the sins you are guilty of, *He can*, and He will! No sin is so severe or so great that He cannot erase it with the blood that Jesus shed on the cross for you. I too felt unworthy and undeserving of His love and forgiveness, but be assured that the same God who can give you the miracle you seek today can forgive and cleanse you from all the sin in your life if you'll just pray with sincerity to Him for His forgiveness.

The scriptures tell us a wonderful story about the pureness of Jesus's intent to save us. In Mark, Jesus says, "I came not to call the righteous, but sinners to repentance," and "sinners" includes you and me![191]

God's grace is greater than anything we have done, and it's by His grace that we are set free from the weight of our sin.

So right now, before you put this book down to begin your search for a bodily miracle, why not accept an even greater miracle for your eternal soul and accept Jesus Christ as your Lord and Savior? Nowhere in scripture is there a specific prayer that details what we need to say to accept Jesus as our Savior, because what is needed is not a series of words or a prayer but rather an acceptance of Christ as your personal Savior and a commitment to turning in a new direction. I have had the great honor and blessing of leading many in accepting Christ, and I would consider it an honor to lead you *right now*! Don't delay; Jesus is calling you at this very moment. The scriptures admonish us not to wait, because none of us is promised tomorrow. In 2 Corinthians 6:2 we read, "behold, *now* is the day of salvation."[192] God's grace is greater than anything we have done, and it's by His grace that we are set free from the weight of our sin.

While there are no particular words you need to say, here is one way that you can pray to accept Christ and be forgiven of all your sin. Simply pray, with a sincere heart, "Lord, I know that I have sinned and that You cannot allow my sin into Your presence. So, Lord, I repent and turn from my sin and ask You to forgive me. Your word tells me that *"all* have sinned" and come short of Your glory, and I believe in Your promise that if I "confess with my mouth the Lord Jesus, and believe in my heart that you [God] raised Him from the dead," that I will be saved.[193] Lord, I do believe in and confess Jesus, and I invite Him into my heart as I accept Him right now as my Lord and my Savior. Help me now, Lord, as I accept the miracle of salvation. Walk with me as I begin my new journey with You, and

---

[191] Mark 2:17 (KJV).

[192] (KJV), emphasis added.

[193] Rom. 3:23, 10:9 (KJV), emphasis added.

teach me Your way. I love You, Lord, and I thank You for loving me and forgiving me. In Jesus's name, I pray. Amen!"

If you prayed this prayer from your heart, congratulations! You just received the greatest miracle of all from God! Your name is now written down in the Lamb's book of life, and the angels in heaven are rejoicing.[194]

Now trust God as you take your first steps toward receiving *your* own miracle!

As Luke 1:37 reminds us, "For with God nothing shall be impossible."[195]

---

[194] Rev. 21:27.
[195] KJV

# ABOUT THE AUTHOR

D<small>R. ROBERT W. LITTKE IS</small> a nationally known author and speaker. Growing up in a Christian household in Southwestern Michigan he accepted Christ at the age of twenty-two. He holds a PhD in counseling psychology. He is a commissioned minister in the Wesleyan Church and is presently the Assistant Pastor of Light and Life Wesleyan Church in Three Rivers, Michigan. He lives in southern Michigan with his wife, Jennifer, and has one daughter and a grandson. For twenty-five years he has been the president and CEO of one of the largest companies in America that provides services to help older adults remain independently in their own homes.

In addition, Dr. Littke worked for over twelve years in radio and television broadcasting, is a highly trained scuba diver who holds the ratings of rescue diver and Divemaster, has worked for over forty years as a deputy sheriff for the county sheriff's department, is an FAA-licensed pilot with almost thirty-five years of flying experience, was appointed by Governor John Engler to the Michigan Commission on Services to the Aging, and has served as president of both his local United Way Directors Council as well as the Michigan Directors of Services to the Aging.

# CONTACT INFORMATION

I F YOU WOULD LIKE TO contact Dr. Littke to share your testimony, to let him know that you have accepted Christ as a result of reading this book, or to have him join you in prayer for your own miracle, you may contact him by using the address listed below or via his website.

Robert W. Littke, PhD
PO Box 8
Nottawa, Michigan 49075

www.MyOwnMiracle.com

Printed in the United States
By Bookmasters